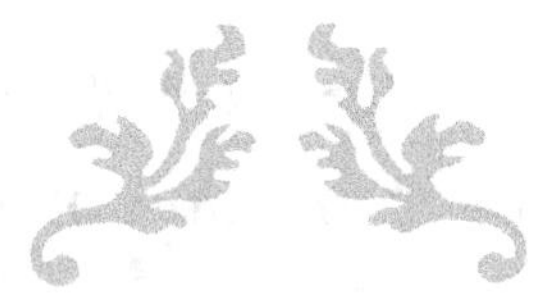

EMOTIONALLY HEALTHY SPIRITUALITY & EMOTIONAL AGILITY WORKBOOK TO MANAGE SELF ESTEEM

Social Emotional Learning : How to Win Loneliness; Create Empathy, Emotional Intelligence and Own Depression Cure

Caryl R. Breton

Contents

11 pm 2

Penn Mar Ave, California. 2

Chapter 1: "I'm like you even if you don't know it." 19

Chapter 2: When the nights are blue and there's no meaning to it 37

Chapter 3: The Global Crisis of Mental Health 55

Chapter 4: The advent of empathy and emotional intelligence in our lives 66

Chapter 5: Emotional intelligence in design and marketing 84

Chapter 6: The Black Dog 96

11 pm

Penn Mar Ave, California.

Sometimes you break. It is not only bodies that are vulnerable to blows. Life sometimes mistreats you. And it doesn't depend on what you do, how much you put in on your part. Resilience is also finite. Then you come undone. Although, of course, as with objects, sometimes you crack inside, even if the eye does not see it.

And then, at another point and for hardly significant reasons, the cracks in your being say that they no longer support more weight. When it starts, it may be nothing more than an intense feeling of discomfort. A kind of omnipresent restlessness that accompanies you wherever you go and stays with you, whatever you do.

You feel that something is wrong, although you cannot identify it. It is a state of restlessness that deprives you of calm. Unhappiness does not go away, and that clouds your pleasant moments. It is that unbearable feeling of wanting everything to end, for the present to disappear, for the moment to cease to be eternal. It is displeasure that gnaws at your insides. You stop sleeping.

Of all its manifestations, this, perhaps, is the cruelest because you stop dreaming. At least before you ran away from yourself at night. There is no more peace or oasis possible. You cannot disconnect from your thoughts; you do not escape discomfort.

Not even exhaustion breaks you as a refuge from that restlessness that burns you. At first, you stop enjoying yourself. Nothing satisfies you; everything irritates you. But it doesn't stop there. I don't know how to explain how it works, nor am I clear why it happens, but it is infallible: spiritual pain builds a physical shell for you. Not as a metaphor.

The surface of the skin dies. When you realize it, you already have the body of a zombie. You look at the ground and think: "Where did all that blood come from? What happened?". And then you discover that you have a glass nailed to the sole of your foot, you don't know for how long.

You remove it, and it doesn't hurt. You cook, you burn with oil, you blister, but you only know it because you see it. Touch does not respond. And the physical numbness seems proportional to the depth of the well. The deeper you are, the less you feel. The more it tears you apart from the inside, the more you disconnect from the outside. The deeper you are, the less you feel!

And with the ability to feel, your energies go away. Depression is a deficit of life, a void of being. And this lack, when it becomes present, empties everything. Because depression also has its peak, the point where existence breaks down.

At that moment, what we call identity becomes an empty facade, a farce. And I don't mean here that you are experiencing an identity crisis like the one that usually occurs in adolescence. It is not an evolution. It is dissolution.

You continue because you have built yourself an automatic pilot. Whether we know it or not, we have many automatisms, habits, even complex cognitive resources that continue to function on their own. But existing becomes unbearable.

How do you explain who has not been through something like that you want to end your life? Living is an instinct; they tell you. But so is avoiding suffering. Because putting a stop to pain is what moves you to do it. Imagine an agony that does not stop, that becomes unbearable, and to which you do not see the end. That is an episode of major depression. Once you fall beyond the edge of the abyss, down the ravine, you live like a doomed Prometheus. Perpetual suffering from which you can only escape by killing yourself.

Depression hurts. And it's not a metaphor. Suffering is not an abstraction. It's bad. You feel it in your chest, in your head, in your gut. That omnipresent discomfort and the feeling that it will always be this way. It is no coincidence that the two groups with the highest risk of suicide, attempted or completed, are major depression and those who live with chronic (physical) pain. Continual suffering is unsustainable.

Of course, major depression can come through. That is why we talk about episodes. Now at that moment, you don't know it, you don't believe it, you can't even conceive it. When you are inside, there is no end to suffering.

Perhaps when you recover, you can proudly say, "I survived myself." But at that moment, in full depression, it is unthinkable. You do not find motives or strength to bear so much suffering. No one can convince you that the blows will stop hurting in the middle of a beating. You just want them to end. Already. This is how a suicide attempt comes along.

How can it happen that you feel bad, feel the suffering, become aware that you are undone, and do not ask for help? Now, looking back, it's easy to explain. It is a stigma, and it is machismo. But when it is happening, you do not even suspect that your prejudices can drag you down the ravine, that they are a source of suffering, and affect your health.

Understanding why it happens is simple: we are not impervious to social prejudice. We look at ourselves in the mirror of the gaze of others. And if the social imaginary teaches us that receiving a mental health diagnosis, taking psychiatric drugs, or even worse, going through a psychiatric hospital stay is something for crazy people or emotionally weak people, it is clear that you are not "that."

You are not looking for help because you are scared to be diagnosed. Prejudice is a serious health problem. Because of it, you arrive at the services when you are already in a crisis, you have more difficulties recovering, and you may end up much worse in your process.

And concerning depression, precisely, gender-dependent differences can be explained in terms of stereotypes of sexual roles. Although there is a greater propensity to label women with depression, men are usually diagnosed when we have more severe symptoms. I was no exception. The fear of the labor and social consequences that the label could bring me was also a strong reason not to ask for help.

Now, empowered and overcome with fear and shame, I can say, as I always do, that it should come as no surprise that I am an individual living with a diagnosis of severe mental disorder; that no person, regardless of their training, trade or profession is free from the possibility of experiencing a mental health problem.

Education can bring us many things, but it does not immunize against suffering. Now, of course, looking back, I can position myself from the security of a life that also continues professionally. Back then, this security was inconceivable. Returning to the world, once broken and labeled, is scary.

Back home, it took me more than two months to get out of a room. Beyond the weight of the symptoms and the over-medication, there was a lot of fear of what awaited me outside in this confinement.

Only in a space that enables and promotes being responsible for oneself and one's community is it possible to abandon the sick person's role and become empowered. Psychoeducation geared towards taking your medication is empowering; learning to iron is empowering; painting mandalas, taking a guided tour of the zoo, listening to a talk about empowerment, everything empowers. Of course, always, always, these are activities offered by professionals for users. Power, of course, comes from above.

Now, in concrete terms, what is empowerment? How do you get it? According to Rappaport's definition: "Empowerment is a process, the mechanism by which people, organizations and communities acquire dominion over their lives."

It is clear, therefore, that painting mandalas do not grant control over our existence. Nor is learning basic skills for personal autonomy empowering. Even the simple act of making decisions does not have this effect.

If that were the case, every time they ask us if we want chicken or meat dürum, they would be empowering us, choosing the movie for the next Netflix Party or the site for the next excursion are not elections that meet the conditions to empower people.

Something more is needed. In this regard, by specifically defining the elements of empowerment in mental health, Judi Chamberlin stressed that empowerment does not only have decision-making power but that these decisions should make it possible to effect changes in one's life and the community. The need for self-management, without labels or people acting as professionals, is precisely to dismantle the reciprocal game that perpetuates the sick role.

The path of activism looks different. It is no longer about breaking prejudices and showing that the first person's associative movement is possible, effective, and transformative. Towards the same horizon, along parallel paths, we have been growing different people and entities. Today it is not all desert or hostile land.

It is no longer just a matter of building a refuge in which to find ourselves, remake ourselves, and recover. Shame has become vindication. It is no longer a personal search. In that sense, I think I have found all that I had lost.

Helen

"I could expect it from someone else, but not from you," I replied when she told me.

I had said it with good intentions, claiming her strength and her profession, but anxiety does not work like that. It can affect anyone, just like so many other diseases.

The following account shares the story of my sister, Helen, and her long battle with anxiety. I bring her story as an overarching reference to my book's central idea and the ever-forgotten aspect of mental health, its wild spontaneity, and its labyrinth.

I am a psychologist, and I suffer from anxiety, yes.

On September 11 of last year, I suffered my first panic attack. At the time, it was not clear to me what was happening to me. Yes, now it is. But let us start at the beginning. It was a normal day. It was no worse than other days.

What's more, it was one of the best moments of that year – he had asked me out just two days ago!! – everything was as good as it could be. However, that morning, while I was working, I had coffee – the second in the morning – like many other days.

When I finished the cup, I began to feel dizzy, breathing difficulties, chest tightness, tachycardia, sweaty hands, fear of fainting, having a stroke, a heart attack. Terror. Fear of dying. All of this accompanied by the fear of fainting in public, ultimately losing control of myself and my body. Coffee wasn't the culprit, of course.

Think of six people in your environment. Keep them in your memory. Now consider that, according to the available estimates, one of those six people will suffer at some point in their life an anxiety disorder:

- *Panic attacks*
- *Agoraphobia*
- *Specific phobias*
- *Social phobia*

- *Generalized anxiety disorder*
- *Post-traumatic stress disorder*
- *Acute stress disorder*
- *Obsessive-compulsive disorder*
- *Unspecified anxiety disorder*

With this personal account, I do not intend to give keys to overcome a disorder of this type, nor will I offer magic recipes. My claim is more modest: to help normalize a disorder that can affect us all, either directly or close people. And within that 'everyone,' of course, mental health professionals are not excluded.

And yes, I am a psychologist, and I have suffered (suffer) from an anxiety disorder. In principle, my training should not be relevant in this, but perhaps it is surprising that one of the phrases that I have heard the most in recent months has been, "do you have anxiety being a psychologist?" You know who asked that one.

When I was in the mood to answer, my answer was, "to think that a psychologist cannot suffer from some kind of mental health problem is like thinking that a doctor cannot catch a cold." Neither psychologists nor any other professional is exempt from suffering health problems. In my case, I discovered that I did not seem to have more tools than the common man to cope with this disorder.

A few years ago, a very close friend began to suffer from anxiety problems. I allowed myself the luxury of giving him some advice – to see a mental health professional, do relaxation techniques, etc. – but when it was my turn, I could not apply any of that advice. And it is that, as they say, "in the house of a blacksmith, a wooden knife."

I would be lying if I said that the first panic attack was the beginning of my anxiety problems, just as it was not the worst part of this process. It all started about two years ago.

At first, the anxiety presented with mild symptoms: isolated nights and distant in time. The physical symptoms were difficulty falling asleep, the sensation of having a stiff jaw and difficulty swallowing.

However, other types of symptoms distressed me more: I felt dizzy, and I was afraid to fall asleep, in case I had some kind of attack, a stroke, a stroke, and I died during the night without knowing it. I was afraid of falling asleep and never waking up again. Anguish and fear kept me awake until I fell asleep from sheer exhaustion.

It was not difficult for me to realize that they were symptoms of anxiety. No, I knew it very soon, probably due to my training, but that did not make me give it the importance it deserved. On the one hand, I did not want to accept that it was possible that I had a problem of this type and, on the other, I believed that it was something temporary and I could control it myself. That was my first mistake.

This situation lasted for months: when I was out of work and had difficulty finding it, another time when I suffered from emotional disappointment, etc. My discomfort, sleepless nights, and dizziness that I did not know where they came from just after consuming exciting things (coffee, soda, etc.) worsened slightly with the diagnosis and progress of the terminal illness of one of the most important people of my life – my late best friend, Rory.

I have always been a very sensitive person; my family and friends laugh at me because I cry about everything. However, throughout his illness and after his death, I was not able to cry. I was completely blank and was unable to explain my emotions or accept what had happened.

Finding the cause of what happens to us is not easy. There is not a single one, and we do not have a way to find it, but I think this situation was the last straw. My fear of dying myself, or one of the people I love, increased, and appeared at the most unexpected moments and in the most varied way.

When I least expected it, fear attacked me and left me frozen and paralyzed. Even today, I don't know how to explain the feeling of cold in my stomach, as if all the blood was suddenly lost. I remember a time when I was walking down the street in high heels. I began to think that I might trip, not keep my balance, fall, and smash my head against the ground. It was not just the thought that it might happen, but real fear, which paralyzed me,

Some everyday situations, such as taking the subway, began to worry me about the risk of having an accident. I stopped reading newspapers or watching the news because every news about accidents or unexpected deaths distressed me thinking that it could happen to me too. These thoughts were presented with intense fear, sweaty hands, and some tachycardia. Also, around that time, I began to experience more and more difficulty sleeping.

In any case, those moments were brief. When I was distracted, I forgot them, so, although it worried me enough to discuss the situation with my family, I did not seek professional help either. I just took herbal remedies to try to sleep better and waited for it to go away on its own.

Second – and more serious – mistake.

That situation continued for a little over a month. After that, I went through a brief period in which I felt good, could sleep easily, and was not plagued by catastrophic thoughts. The period was very short, but I trusted myself, and I assumed that whatever was happening to me had already been solved and that, although I had come to consider it, I no longer needed professional help.

A few weeks later, I had my first panic attack.

As I write it, I wonder how I could not realize how serious the situation was and how much help I needed, but I was not, and being a psychologist did not facilitate it.

The same day of the first panic attack, moved by intense fear and uncontrollable anguish that I felt, I located a psychologist with training that convinced me and requested an appointment three days later.

Suffering from this situation and being overwhelmed made me understand that I needed help and could not control it alone. The fear of never getting over the situation by myself was what finally moved me. I didn't want to; I couldn't go through something like that again.

In addition to seeking psychological help, I went to my family doctor, referred from the emergency department, where I ended up after the first attack, where they used Lorazepam to control my attack. She proposed a drug treatment to me that, at first, I did not want to follow.

Two days after the first panic attack, I suffered the second while at home. Despite knowing what was happening to me and that it had happened to me before without major consequences, I could not handle it, and, again, I had to resort to Lorazepam since fear overwhelmed me. I still did not have the necessary tools to cope without drug help.

The worst was not the panic attacks, but the general state I found myself in each day after that second attack. I was constantly dizzy like it was on a boat, or the ground was completely uneven. I was distracted, tired, unable to pay attention, constantly aware of my condition, scared of having another attack. Fear did not give up. Fear and anguish.

I wasn't able to pay attention to the people around me. I went out with my friends or my family members, and I could not follow their conversations because discomfort and fear barely let me out of myself. I have forgotten the entire conversations and situations of those months.

And it's not that I didn't exactly remember the conversations, but they did ring a bell, but I don't remember that they happened at all. I have forgotten to have seen movies, have listened to songs, etc., totally completely. For months, I have been looking at myself for a dark part that haunted me.

And inside me, the recurring thoughts. They attacked me, and I was not able to control them. All related to death or accidents, with when and how I was going to die, with which all my relatives and loved ones would one day be gone, and I did not know when would be the last time I would see them.

Imagine the anguish that seeing your loved ones triggers the thought of whether that's the last time you'll see them. I got to the point where I passed people on the street, and I only thought about the years that those people had lived. I calculated how old they should be, and I thought that I was capable too if they had reached that age.

I thought over and over about the moment when it was time to die. I was afraid of getting old because I was approaching death. I wondered what it would be like if I would be afraid, or if I was older, I would no longer be. We all know that one day the people we love, and we will no longer be there, but we live day by day without thinking about it. However, for me, it was as if what I had always known that someone was there suddenly was lighting it up with a very powerful spotlight, and it was no longer able to look at anything else. The truth is that I feared that I would never be able to recover or fall into a depression.

During the first weeks, I have already mentioned it, I preferred not to take too much Lorazepam even though my doctor had recommended it to me. Professionally, I have always defended the combination of psychotherapy and controlled use of medication. Still, when it was my turn, I fell into the same prejudices as other people, and I was afraid of getting hooked, becoming tolerant, and needing more and more, etc. I tried treating myself only with psychotherapy, but most nights, I needed a sock or a pill to get to sleep.

The nights were, without a doubt, the worst time. I would arrive at nine o'clock at night with very high tension, I was shaking uncontrollably, and I was short of breath. It was like being terrified without interruption.

Once, on vacation with my partner, I found myself in the car shaking with fear, without him being able to do anything to comfort me, and nothing had happened. Anxiety and a feeling of loss of control go hand in hand. Fear gripped me, prevented me from eating, made me shiver as if I were freezing to death. Think of the most intense fear you have ever felt and imagine that it lasts for hours or even days.

Finally, I accepted the advice of my GP, whom I thank for her good work since from the first moment she treated me with respect, seriousness, and concern, and I began to take some medication – always under medical supervision and indication – at midafternoon to reach the calmer night.

Stopping feeling that intense and constant fear, thanks to the medication, helped me relax and take advantage of the therapy much more and better since I could finally begin to concentrate.

As for psychotherapy, it was very intense and deep work. It started by realizing that the anxiety did not come on suddenly but was due to my behavior patterns, stress management, coping with problems, lack of self-esteem, etc. And that not everything was limited to recent situations, but a whole history of the need for control, lack of assertiveness, low self-esteem, and problems of confidence in my abilities.

They were due to a catastrophic personality very focused on everything that could go wrong. Recent stressful situations have only pushed me to the limit.

The personal work of self-knowledge and change that I had to carry out during the time that the therapy lasted was not easy, nor was it free of pain, but I felt accompanied by my psychologist, by my family members, and by my friends, who from the first moment they knew what was happening to me.

I had to be very constant and put all my willpower into making an effort to take advantage of the therapy, carry out the proposals that my psychologist made me, and not give up even if it took time to see results.

Also, talking about my situation with my loved ones was very helpful as I discovered how many people had been through it, even within my closest family, without my knowing it. The testimony and support of others who had traveled a path similar to mine was helpful.

Almost a year has passed, and my anxiety has not disappeared or the personal work that I have to do every day has finished, but it no longer dominates me, it does not keep me sleepless every night, and it does not condition me.

Every day is an effort to keep changing and improving my behavior patterns and the negative thoughts that come upon me, but now I have the necessary tools and the motivation to do so, and I know that if I need to, I can go to my psychologist again. I have not completely changed my old habits, but now I am aware of what I was doing and doing to myself, and that helps me to be able to stop and look for different options. Therapy and personal work have made me aware of multiple avoidant attitudes and behaviors that I was carrying out without even realizing it.

As I said initially, no one is free from suffering from any type of illness, regardless of their profession, but anxiety disorders can be improved and managed with professional help. In my case, the help of psychotherapy and medication was necessary.

Each one should look for the option that best suits their needs but always seek professional help. It can be controlled; you can not only regain your normal life but improve it. But you cannot and do not have to do it alone. It does not matter if you are a psychologist, housewife, or astronaut.

We need help, and we must seek it both in our primary care medical center, where your family doctor will assess whether to treat you or refer you to the psychiatrist, as well as in a psychologist specialized in anxiety disorders.

Why I decided to write this book?

For most of my life, two mysteries hung over me. I didn't understand them, and if I'm honest, I was scared to investigate them. The first mystery is that I am in my 30s, and throughout my life, depression and anxiety have increased throughout the Western world.

I wanted to understand: why is this happening to us? Why is it so hard for so many more of us to get through the day?

And I wanted to understand this for a more personal mystery. When I was a teenager, I went to my doctor, and I remember telling him that I felt the pain was escaping me. I couldn't control it; I was quite ashamed of it.

My doctor told me a story that I now see was not wrong but rather simplified. He said, "we know why people feel this way. Sometimes something goes wrong in people's brains. There is a natural chemical imbalance. All we need to do is give you a drug to get your chemicals back to normal. So he gave me an antidepressant.

And I felt a lot better for a while, I had a real boost, but then the depression came back. So they gave me higher and higher doses until, for 13 years, I was taking the maximum dose possible but still had a lot of pain. So, I started to wonder: "I'm doing everything they tell me to do; Why do I keep feeling like this? "

I interviewed leading scientific experts and people who have been through depression everywhere. I learned that there is scientific evidence for nine factors that lead to our depression. Two of them are, in fact, in our biology.

Your genes can make you more sensitive to these problems, and there are real changes in the brain that occur when you get depressed that can make it harder to get out. But most of the factors that have been shown to cause depression and anxiety are not in our biology.

For example, if you are lonely, you are much more likely to become depressed. If you are in control at work, you are much more likely to get depressed. If you don't interact with the natural world, you are much more likely to become depressed. These are factors of the way we live, and once you understand them, a very different set of solutions opens up that must be offered alongside the option of drugs.

We all know that we have natural physical needs. You need food, shelter, water, and clean air. There is equally strong evidence that all human beings have natural psychological needs. You need to feel that you belong. You need to feel that your life has meaning and purpose.

This culture we have built is good at many things, but we are becoming less and less good at meeting people's deep underlying psychological needs.

Some part of my book asks what the unmet psychological needs leading to this epidemic of depression and anxiety are. And so how can we begin to build a culture that meets those needs?

Our clinical system is created to respond mainly to biological problems. There are some real biological causes of depression, but they exist alongside and interact with these huge psychological and social causes.

I'll start by giving you an example. Everyone knows that junk food has taken over our diet and made us physically sick. I'm not saying this with any superiority. I came here from McDonald's. But there is equally strong evidence that some kind of junk values have taken over our minds and made us mentally ill.

For thousands of years, philosophers have said, "If you think life is about money, and status, and display, you're going to feel like shit." It is not an exact quote from Confucius, but it is the gist of what he said. But strangely, no one had scientifically proven this until an amazing man I met named Professor Tim.

His research suggests crucial insights. The more you think that life is about buying things and showing them and how you see yourself to other people, the more likely you are to get depressed and anxious in a significant amount. And as a society, we have become *much* more driven by these forces.

At first, this seems pretty obvious. Everyone knows that you will not lie on your deathbed and think about all the likes you have on Instagram and all the shoes you bought. You will think of moments of love and connection.

But, as Professor Tim told me, we live in a machine designed so that we neglect what is important in life. We are constantly bombarded with messages telling us to look for happiness in the wrong places.

Professor Tim wanted to find out if we can disrupt that machine. He did an experiment in which he had people come together, once every few weeks, for months, to talk about the times when they have found meaning and purpose in their lives.

For some people, it was playing music or running on the beach with their children. The group was designed to ask – how can you spend more of your life on these things and less on these junk values?

They showed that only this experience led to a significant change in people's values. It alienated them from the forces that caused so much depression.

These are causes that go far beyond our biology, and our current medical system is not good at responding to non-biological causes.

I think it is too simplistic to say that these causes "respond to the dynamics of capitalist life."

First of all, several of them, like childhood traumas, have nothing to do with capitalism. And secondly, in communist societies like the Soviet Union and North Korea, there was an enormous amount of depression, despair, and anxiety, almost certainly more than in our societies.

Any kind of economy – capitalist, communist, social-democratic – can fail to meet people's underlying human needs if it doesn't work well. The core problem is that many of the deepest needs of people as humans are not being met by how our society works right now.

But to address your question. If you don't understand what causes a problem, it is really difficult to solve. So far, most people have been offered a very simplistic story about their depression. They say it is solely and entirely a problem with your brain chemistry.

That only leads to one solution: drugs. The drugs give some relief, but for most, sadly, they are not solving the problem in the long run. The best scientific research shows that most people who take chemical antidepressants become depressed again. So, we need to have a deeper understanding of the problem to expand the menu of solutions.

For example?

In 2000, a South African psychiatrist named Derek Summerfield was in Cambodia doing some research on the psychological effects of unexploded landmines, at a time when chemical antidepressants were being marketed for the first time in the country.

Local doctors didn't know much about these drugs, so they asked Summerfield to explain them. When he finished, they explained that they didn't need these new chemicals because they already had antidepressants.

Puzzled, Derek asked them to explain, hoping they would tell him about some local herbal remedy. Instead, they told him about something quite different.

They told him a story about a farmer they had treated. He was working in the rice fields, and one day he stepped on a landmine and had his leg blown off. They put an artificial limb on him, and eventually, he went back to work.

But it is very painful to work when your joint is underwater, and returning to the field where it was blown up made him very anxious. He became deeply depressed.

Doctors and his neighbors sat down with this man and talked about his life and his problems. They realized that even with his new artificial limb, his old job was too difficult, that he was constantly stressed and in physical pain, and that these things combined to simply want to stop living.

His interlocutors had an idea. They suggested that he work as a milkman, a job that would cause less pain for his false leg and produce fewer disturbing memories. They believed that he was perfectly capable of making the switch. So they bought him a cow.

In the months and years that followed, his life changed. His depression, which was once deep, lifted. Cambodian doctors told Dr. Summerfield, "You see, doctor, the cow was an antidepressant."

Over time, I came to believe that this little scene in Southeast Asia, which at first sounds a bit quirky, actually represents, in a distilled way, a change in perspective that many of us have to make if we want to progress.

Only because they understood the cause of the farmer's depression could they find the solution. So we have to ask ourselves: what is causing our depression, and what is the cow for that?

I have seen the answer to this question put into practice. We are the loneliest society in the history of mankind. A recent study asked Americans, "how many people know you well?" Half of them said no one.

It's not that bad in America, but it's getting worse. I spent a lot of time talking to a man named Professor John in Chicago, the world's leading expert on solitude. He said to me – why do we exist? Everyone in this room, all of us?

One reason is that our ancestors in the savannas of Africa were very good at one thing. They weren't bigger than the animals they shot down; they weren't faster than the animals they shot down, but they were much better at grouping together and cooperating. Just as bees evolved to live in a hive, humans evolved to live in a tribe.

We are the first humans to try to dissolve our tribes.

But there is a solution. One of my heroes is a doctor named Sam Everington. He is a general practitioner in a poor area of East London, where I lived for a long time, and he was very uncomfortable. He had many patients who came to him with depression, and like me, he is not opposed to chemical antidepressants, which for some people, are an advantage, but he could see that for many of his patients, they were not solving their problems. So one day, he decided to try something different.

A woman came into his office named Lisa Cunningham. I met her later. Lisa had been locked up at home with paralyzing depression and anxiety for seven years. He had barely left his house. Sam said, "Don't worry, I'll keep giving you these drugs." But I'm also going to prescribe something else.

There was an area behind the medical office suite that was just a bare lot. Sam said to Lisa, "What I would like you to do is come and go, a few times a week, to this lot, and meet with a group of other depressed and anxious people to find something meaningful to do together."

The first time the group met, Lisa was physically ill. But the group started talking, and they asked: what can we do? And they decided that they were going to build a garden. They were people from central East London like me who didn't know anything about gardening. So they started reading books, watching videos.

They began to put their fingers in the ground. They began to learn the rhythms of the seasons. There is much evidence that exposure to the natural world is a very powerful antidepressant.

But they started to do something even more important. They began to form a tribe. They began to form a group. They began to worry about each other. If one of them didn't show up, they'd go looking for them.

As Lisa told me, when the garden began to bloom, we began to bloom. This approach is called social prescribing, and there is a growing body of evidence showing that it produces substantial drops in depression and anxiety.

In this culture, we are constantly told, when we feel anxious or depressed, to be you. Be yourself. As if individualism is what we should be looking for. But, what depression taught me is, don't be you. Don't be yourself. Let's be us. Let's be us. What we should aspire to is to be part of a tribe.

The most important thing is to explain to people that if you are depressed or anxious, that you are not weak. He is not mad. He is not, in general, a machine with broken parts. He is a human being with unmet needs and what he deserves is love and support to meet those deepest needs. Once you understand this, you can begin to solve some of the problems that cause so much depression.

We can ask people if they hate their job. There is strong evidence that human beings need to feel that our lives have meaning, that we are doing something with a purpose that makes a difference. It is a natural psychological need. But between 2011 and 2012, the Gallup polling company conducted the most detailed study ever conducted of how people feel that we spend most of our waking lives doing our paid work.

They found that 13% of people say they are "committed" to their work, find it meaningful, and look forward to it. 63% say they are "not engaged," which is defined as "sleepwalking on their workday." And 24% are "actively offline" – they hate it.

Most of the depressed and anxious people I know, I realized, are in the 87% who don't like their job. So, I started inquiring to see if there is any evidence that this could be related to depression. It turned out that an Australian scientist named Michael Marmott had made a breakthrough in answering this question in the 1970s.

He wanted to investigate what causes stress in the workplace, and he believed he had found the perfect laboratory to discover the answer: British civil service, based in Whitehall.

This small army of bureaucrats and officials was divided into nineteen different layers, from the Permanent Secretary at the top to the typists at the bottom. What I wanted to know, at first, was:

Everyone told him: you're wasting your time. The boss is going to be more stressed because he has more responsibility. But when Michael published his results, he revealed that the exact opposite was true. The lower an employee is in the hierarchy, the higher their stress level, and the likelihood of having a heart attack. Now I wanted to know: why?

And that's when, after two more years studying officials, he discovered the biggest factor. It turns out that if you have no control over your work, you are much more likely to get stressed and, more importantly, to get depressed.

Humans have an innate need to feel that what we are doing daily is meaningful. When you are in control, you cannot create meaning from your work.

Suddenly, the depression of many of my friends, even those with fancy jobs, who spend most of their waking hours feeling controlled and unappreciated, started to seem like not a problem with their brains, but a problem with their environments.

I learned that there are many causes of depression like this. But my journey was not simply about finding the reasons why we feel so bad. The core was figuring out how we can feel better and find real, long-lasting antidepressants that work for most of us, beyond the pill packs we've been offered so often as the only menu item for the depressed and the anxious. We have to deal with the deeper issues that are causing all this anguish.

You decided that you consciously and deliberately wanted to take steps to be a happier person. Let's say you decided to spend two hours a day being happier. They wanted to find out. Does doing that make you happier? Works? They studied this in four countries: the United States, Russia, Japan, and Taiwan.

And what they found out was that at first, it looked really weird. If you consciously try to make yourself happier in the United States, you don't become happier. But in other countries, if you try to make yourself happier, you do it. They were averages. There were exceptions.

Why would that be? What is happening here? They went and studied it more. They found that in America, in general, if you try to make yourself happier, you do something for yourself. You buy something; you work harder for a promotion, you treat yourself, whatever it is.

In other countries, in general, if you try to make yourself happier, you do something for another person, your friends, your family, your community. So, we have an implicitly individualistic story about happiness. They have an implicit collectivist story about happiness. And it turns out that our vision of happiness doesn't work. Some kind of individualists would have died in the savannas of Africa.

And after he explained it to me, I realized that my story about happiness had been wrong for a long time. When I felt these painful feelings approaching, I met them with some individual accomplishment, buying something for myself, doing something "awesome" at work, doing some kind of external accomplishment. And it rarely worked. It rarely made me happier.

When I feel those painful feelings coming (and sometimes I do), I try to do something for someone else. It can be as simple as leaving my phone at home, visiting them, and listening to them. In a society where people are so lonely, being heard is an incredible gift.

And this simple change, of realizing that my happiness can only come from boosting others' happiness, has had a strong effect on me.

All of that is very important. To progress, we need to start by changing our understanding of what depression and anxiety are. There are very real biological contributions to depression and anxiety.

But if we allow biology to become the big picture, implicitly telling people: your pain means nothing. It's a wiring problem in your brain, like a glitch in a computer program.

I could only begin to change my life when I learned that your depression is not a problem. It is a sign. Your pain makes sense. You feel that way for reasons, and those reasons can be addressed. It took me a long time to conclude, but the message from the scientists and the crisis around us is increasingly clear. We have to stop insulting these signals and start listening to them because they tell us something we need to hear.

As a culture, we have become deeply individualistic. It has trained us to seek happiness in all the wrong places.

I had a pretty bad depression for a long time, from my teens. I experienced pretty severe abuse from an adult as a child. I never wanted to think about this or talk about it. I didn't want to give this individual power over me now.

In writing my book, I interviewed leading experts who have shown how childhood traumas can cause depression and all kinds of problems in adults, like obesity and addiction.

And they taught me something very important that they had found in their research. It is not the abuse that destroys you. It is a shame of abuse. And if you can find safe places to release the shame you feel, that can free you from your depression.

People who suffer abuse in childhood tend to internalize the voice of their abuser. They think that they do not deserve to be treated with love and care. A safe and loving connection that helps you release your shame helps release those abusive voices from your mind.

Evidence shows that reducing shame heals you deeply and can reduce your depression and anxiety.

For more than 30 years, we have told, as a culture, a primal story about depression and anxiety, and that story has come to dominate the discussion.

When I was a teenager, I went to my doctor and explained that I felt the anguish coming out of me uncontrollably, like a foul smell. He told me a story. He said that depression is caused by the spontaneous lack of a chemical in the brain called serotonin. I simply needed to take some medications to raise my serotonin levels to a normal level.

Recently, a young friend of one of my nephews, not much older than I was when I was first diagnosed, went to his doctor and asked for help with his depression. Your doctor told you that you had a problem with *dopamine* in your brain. In 20 years, all that has changed is the name of the chemical.

I believed and predicted this story for more than a decade. But when I started researching the causes of depression and anxiety for my book, I was surprised to find leading scientific organizations saying that this approach was based on a misunderstanding of science. There are actual biological factors that contribute to depression, but they are far from the whole story.

I learned that the World Health Organization explained in 2011: "Mental health occurs socially: the presence or absence of mental health is above all a social indicator and therefore requires social as well as individual solutions."

The United Nations, in its official statement on the occasion of World Health Day in 2017, said that "the dominant biomedical narrative on depression" is based on "the biased and selective use of research results" that "cause more harm than good, undermine the right to health and must be abandoned. There is a "growing evidence base," said the UN authors, that there are deeper causes of depression, so while there is some role for drugs, we need to stop using them "to address issues that are closely related to social problems. We need to move from "focusing on" chemical imbalances "to focusing on" power imbalances."

At first, I was puzzled by statements like this, which went against everything I had been told. So I spent three years interviewing the world's leading scientists on these issues to understand what is going on in places where despair in our culture is worst, from Cleveland to Sao Paulo, and where the incidence of despair is minor, including Amish communities.

I learned that there is broad agreement among scientists that there are three types of causes of depression and anxiety and that all three occur, to varying degrees, in all depressed and anxious people. The causes are: biological (like your genes), psychological (how you think of yourself), and social (the broader ways we live together).

Very few people dispute this. But when it comes to communicating with the public and offering help, psychological solutions have been increasingly neglected, and environmental solutions have been almost totally ignored.

When we understand this problem differently, we can start to find real solutions.

"And here you are living, despite it all." – Rupi Kaur.

This book aims to make known the reality of mental health and basic guidelines that you have to take into account in the performance of all those tasks, which as an individual, are entrusted to you in this area.

Keep in mind that the key to success lies in the bond, the ability to share emotional time and space, accompany what goes beyond the task, where the center is the person attended, and its context.

Do not forget that you are not alone on this path, which is quite a team of which you are part, the one that is focused on following the objective: to keep our mental health in check and improve the quality of life of people affected by it.

We are all in this together.

Chapter 1: "I'm like you even if you don't know it."

Mental health is essentially defined as a state of emotional, mental, and social well-being. It affects the way we think, feel, and act. It determines our interaction with life. How we handle difficult situations, how we interact with other people, and make decisions.

But, the concept of mental health is not absolute. Not having a recognized mental disorder does not necessarily indicate that we will always fail at mental health.

The concept of health is not in black and white – you have it, or you don't have it. It is a matter of degrees. In life, we pass, and we will go through different moments, where we will find different states of physical health and mental health.

We must pay attention and care to our health in a comprehensive way. The type of difficulties and how we face them will determine the appearance or not of some emotional or psychological disorder, and this may be of different types and intensities.

For all this, the concept of mental health should be a natural concept, like physical health, without prejudice or stigma. We all will go through times when we will experience a problem, but that does not mean that we are the problem.

I like the slogan of the Spanish Mental Health Confederation recent campaign on World Mental Health Day: "I'm like you even if you don't know it." It comes to remind us that when we talk about having or not having mental health, we are all in the same "boat." The figures offered by the different epidemiological studies tell us about what mental health is like in the world are staggering.

A European study that was carried out in 2010 that included 30 countries showed data that 38.2%, that is, 164 million people in Europe, had some mental disorder at the time of the study.

It is also essential to pay attention to the data on mental disorders in children and adolescents. Some epidemiological studies indicate that between 7 and 25% of minors meet the criteria for a psychiatric diagnosis.

The most common mental problems or disorders are anxiety, insomnia, and depression. The five mental disorders with the greatest impact are dysthymia, major depressive episode, post-traumatic stress disorders, panic disorder, and social phobia.

Although certain efforts are made, and in the Declaration of Helsinki (European Declaration, 2006), it is urged to promote a shift from attention to mental health services, we still have much to do.

For now, only a small fraction of people with mental health problems receive treatment, and in many cases, with delay or ineffective treatments.

Another large part of the population does not even know that they have a mental illness. As institutions work to improve these care levels, what can we do for ourselves, our friends, and family?

What can we do for our mental health?

First, we can learn to detect our problems and be more aware of them. Having information and more self-awareness is the first step in solving our difficulties.

Many people manage to feel that they are "bad" even "awful." Still, they do not identify this high discomfort with suffering from some disorder, such as depression, a personality disorder, an eating disorder, or an obsessive disorder.

It may seem surprising to us, but it is the reality, and I see it frequently in the office and my environment. Too many people attend to their difficulties with an "I'll get over it" or an "I'm like this."

Either they never attend to those problems, or they delay their attention for up to five or more years. And in the course of the problem, they strive and fight to be better. From the knowledge they have at their fingertips, they apply intuition or allow themselves to be advised by friends, and they live day by day, facing symptoms that make their life.

On many occasions, a true ordeal.

Thus, the first important question in mental health is to have adequate and sufficient information to acquire knowledge and be aware, identify, and prevent problems.

If they are aware of their illness, their problems and have decided to go to a psychologist, psychologist, or psychiatrist. Many people have decided to go to a psychologist, psychologist, or psychiatrist to deal with them.

Even though they have not chosen to be ill and have not made any conscious decisions that have caused their illness, they feel guilty and ashamed and suffer isolation and the effects of a stigma that remains today associated with mental illness.

People naturally accept having a physical illness. We do not feel guilty about it. We share it, we express it, they understand us, and with it, we obtain support from others, and we feel relieved and accompanied.

We all hear people talking about their illnesses as part of the natural, daily conversations in their life. However, in general, we are ashamed; we feel weak, inferior, guilty, incapable, and we hide it.

Throughout these years, more than half of the people I know and talk to, at some point have expressed to me with great sadness, also with helplessness and above all with feelings of loneliness, that they could not share their psychological problems, that they did not understand them, and that they carried their illness in silence, for fear of being seen as weak, of rejection, of dismissal, and also for fear of the banal responses of others, devoid of empathy, generated from the lack of "culture and knowledge about mental health."

Phrases like: "What you have to do is go out and have fun." "It's that you don't make an effort." "You lack the will." "Happiness is a choice." The worst thing is that these comments often convince those who suffer from mental disorders that this is the case.

Having a mental health problem cannot be a secret or embarrassment, but a challenge to achieve our balance.

We all have a person by our side with a mental health problem, or we will have one, according to the figures provided by epidemiological studies. We may have one or more mental health problems throughout our lives. It is time to prepare and move forward in the knowledge of mental illness and understand those who suffer from it.

Let us ask with respect and without judging, seek information from good sources, listen without giving solutions that we do not have, give only support, that in these difficult moments do not feel alone or alone.

A mental health problem cannot be a secret, nor an embarrassment, but a challenge.

It would be good if, from these reflections, we move forward with a mind clear of fear and prejudice towards the construction of better mental health, ours, and everyone's. We develop our emotional capacities to enjoy ourselves and others, our partners and family, and achieve the harmony and well-being we all deserve.

When we enter a hospital or a health center and see the mental health area signposted, or even when we go down the street and see a psychology center advertised, what is the first thing that comes to mind? What do we associate mental health with?

If any of the meanings of the expression "being crazy" is included in your answer, I think we are on the same page.

"Madness" an image full of prejudices

I have been talking to psychologists for years. I have always believed that progress and knowledge would remove prejudices, stereotypes, and stigmas from the field of mental health. And although there has been a significant advance, I still find people who resist going to a psychologist's consultation. If they do, they maintain modest secrecy with their family and friends. Everything is to avoid being considered "crazy"!

The professionals who work in mental health have special care using the word "madness." It is not that we have any taboo on the term, but that they are aware of the "imagery" that around this expression they have created Literature, cinema, or even history itself, with those "controversial" biographies of some "illustrious characters."

In short, everything has contributed to the fact that when we detect any sign that something in our way of thinking or our emotions is not "normal" – and later, we will speak of "normality" – we feel enormous discomfort and fear.

Curiously, in these times, there is a concern that quite the contrary, we usually boast about: physical health. We tell all our family and friends that we go to the gym, that we have started a super diet, that we train our body, and even – if our pockets allow it – that we have a "personal trainer."

And nobody judges us for it. They are more likely to congratulate us.

Doesn't it seem paradoxical to you that we don't feel any shame in training our body, and instead, it doesn't seem convenient to train our mind? Don't you think that we should speak with the same naturalness of aspiring to good mental health to good physical health?

And I can't resist asking one more question. Don't you think that if we have a specialist in the human body for this physical health training, we shouldn't have a specialist of the mind, a psychologist, to train mental health, which is at least the same or more complex?

Aspiring to improve our resources, capacities, and emotional abilities mean learning to think better and relate better. In short, to live happier and more satisfied is not a "crazy" aspiration.

Who goes to see a psychologist?

People come to consultations to train their ability to speak in public, improve their "sleep hygiene," relate and communicate socially in a natural way, be assertive and honest with themselves, have a fuller sexual life, or improve their ability to lead human teams in positions of responsibility.

Do you think these people, with these aspirations, are crazy? Of course not.

There are many examples of people who have adequate functioning in their day to day but decide to request help to improve, change, reflect, decide, etc. In short, take action and overcome new goals. Because every day we are clearer about our well-being, our happiness depends primarily on us, on our behavior, attitude, and thinking.

And here a new prejudice appears: "It's that I'm like that, I can't change."

On many occasions, we believe that happiness depends on our environment, the situation we live in, whether we have health, a partner, money, or work. But did you know that this variable – the situation – only influences our happiness by 10%? And the remaining 90%?

Let's see some data on the perception of happiness.

50% depends on our genetics, our natural tendencies, personality variables, and our biology. And 40% depends on us, on our behavior, on our coping, on our way of handling emotions.

And I'm going to tell you a little secret, in that 40% is where happiness is perceived more intensely. In other words, when we manage to be happy thanks to something that we have achieved, and not something that is given to us, the feeling of happiness is much fuller.

Each of us can increase our well-being, our happiness, by 40%. Don't you think it's worth it? Don't you think all the help is good in this challenge?

What is psychology for?

Part of psychology professionals' work is to guide, discover resources, train, and direct for your great personal challenge, just like when you prepare a long-distance race and have a coach.

Psychologists treat psychopathology, anxiety disorders, depression, personality disorders, or eating behavior disorders. Still, the reasons for consultation not associated with disorders but with imbalances and daily problems of our day are persistent: insomnia, relationship problems, smoking cessation, grief, decision-making, poor control of anger, communication problems with children, self-esteem.

In short, Clinical Psychology is not only science at the service of pathologies. It also has the purpose of helping you discover your personality components and guide you so that you decide what to do with them, what to improve, complement, and overcome. It helps you to become the owner of your emotions, but not by blocking or avoiding them – that's impossible, they have a fundamental role in our life – the goal is to increase the perception of control over them and decide how to act, being fully aware of what we feel. We do, taking control of our life, without being like a weather vane carried away by the wind, by any wind.

There are many myths related to the profession. A few myths about psychology and psychologists:

1. Only those who are weak need help.
2. Psychologists can guess your thoughts. They are like fortune tellers.
3. All those who go to the psychologist are crazy.
4. All psychology professionals have a bad head. They are weird.
5. They brainwash you.
6. They tell you what to do.
7. All psychological treatments are long.
8. If you stop going to the psychologist, your problems come back.

Psychologists are health professionals who are experts in behavior and emotions. They provide strategies to acquire emotional skills and resources that improve the physical and psychological health of the people, always respecting patients' decisions, motivations, and needs. But, what is the line that separates normal from abnormal? When do I know I need help? When do emotions become a problem? When emotions are a sign that something is wrong:

- If they generate psychological discomfort several times a day for an extended period.
- If emotions generate a high physiological activation and it is maintained over time.
- If they negatively affect our health.
- If it hinders our performance.
- If they generate maladaptive behavior (increased arguments, isolation, absenteeism from work, substance abuse, bingeing, etc.).
- If we perceive not having control over them, they dominate us and condition our day to day.

Do not forget that for everyone, knowing our limits is a significant discovery in life. Demanding the right help at the right time is not a sign of weakness, but of intelligence, and also of strength and courage.

Cognitive behavioral therapy. The choice of treatment

"I'm going to improve; I want to go to a psychologist, but... where?" What will they do? How will they do it?

I know, I know that deciding to improve is a great advance. I know that deciding to go to a psychologist is a first step that shows conviction and motivation.

But I also know that from that moment on, questions arise that are not always, and not for all or all, easy to answer: Which psychology center do I go to? What do I have to ask? What type of professional in psychology should I choose? What is this Cognitive Behavioral Therapy thing I've heard about?

The first visit to a psychologist or psychologist is not easy. Many and very diverse are the reasons, feelings, and weaknesses present in those who consider taking the step of receiving psychological treatment.

A feeling that is practically in all of the people who live this experience is that of insecurity. Insecurity in the face of the emotional discomfort they suffer, the impossibility of handling it on their own, and the doubt of what they will find when receiving therapy. As will be? What will they tell me? Will it help me?

In the moments in which we perceive ourselves with more fragility, looking for stable, specific, reliable support is usually the first step, necessary to regain the feeling of control in our day to day, the feeling of security. And there a fundamental question arises:

Can we entrust this professional support to any type of psychological therapy and any psychologist or psychologist? The answer, without a doubt, is the intuited one: no.

I have written this section with a clear objective: to answer the most frequently asked questions – five specifically – asked by people who attend first sessions or take the preliminary interview.

What is cognitive behavioral, psychological treatment?

Cognitive behavioral therapy is a type of psychological therapy that is not based on intuition or personal interpretation of the psychologist or psychologist who directs, but a methodology, a defined system, whose effectiveness and guarantees clinics have been demonstrated and supported by scientific studies.

In this clinical system, the first phase is essential: an evaluation.

The psychological evaluation is carried out through various procedures, the scope, and variety, which will be determined by the reasons for consultation or the aspects that the psychologist appreciates in the first sessions.

Some of these procedures are clinical interviews, evaluation tests or questionnaires, and self-records that the person performs.

Now in which the two active subjects in the treatment:

- A person seeking change.
- A Psychologist who directs it, they agree that it has been clearly understood what is happening, why it is happening, and why the problem remains, it is time to continue with the next phase of treatment: how to change it.

In most psychological practices, they dedicate a session to deliver and explain a written report. All the conclusions drawn in the evaluation phase are exposed.

Such a report includes an explanatory model that details the relationship between the main processes involved in the problem, a series of specific and valuable objectives, and a treatment plan to achieve these objectives.

1.   **What is the choice of some treatment techniques based on and not others?**

And again, I must insist that treatment techniques are never chosen based on the professional's intuition or personal preference. In cognitive behavioral therapy, those techniques and clinical tools are chosen, which have proven to be more effective in changing the dysfunctional processes identified in the evaluation phase.

Comparing it with other health processes, if you have fallen and your arm hurts, I would not do a blood test to evaluate a possible fracture: I would perform an x-ray because it is the appropriate and ideal evaluation procedure for the problem.

And if we see a fracture, I would not prescribe exercises because "I know that will help you" I would recommend immobilization of the arm because studies show that an initial period of immobilization is necessary after a fracture of these characteristics.

In cognitive behavioral therapy, saving distances, we work along the same lines. There is a form of evaluation and treatments established as the most suitable and most effective for each process or psychological problem.

Those of us who work in the Health area have no doubts: let us work with the most adequate and efficient scientific procedures, and not with others!

As Llobell, Frías Navarro, and Monterde i Bor (2004) say: The wide proliferation of psychological treatments that currently exist requires control of their quality and effects.

Not everything goes well when applying a psychological technique or procedure to a person with a series of problems.

2. What is the normal frequency of cognitive behavioral therapy? Will I go every week? When and how does it end?

The frequency of sessions in cognitive behavioral therapy is not something improvised either. Studies have shown that in the first phase, a weekly frequency is the one that obtains the best results and does so in the shortest time.

When the change process begins to stabilize (the proposed objectives begin to be partially achieved), the sessions are separated (once every two weeks, for example). And when the goals are practically achieved, the sessions are even further apart (once a month at first, then once every 2-3 months). In the last phase, called follow-up, what is sought is:

- Strengthen the learned processes that have led to the change.
- Prevent possible relapses.

After some follow-up sessions, the process is finished.

3. What if psychological treatment is not helping me?

Since a treatment plan with objectives is established, from time to time, it is advisable for the psychologist and the patient to spend time sharing and contrasting how and to what extent the objectives are being met.

This sharing is very useful to consolidate and reinforce and reorient, redirect, or introduce the necessary treatment changes.

The fundamental thing is that the person knows that the objective is to overcome the problem and make his change. For this, you will have the professional attention of the psychologist or psychologist who directs your treatment and all the clinical resources, information, and support.

4. How long does a cognitive behavioral treatment last?

It depends. Different manifestations are clear warnings that it is convenient to seek professional help: loss of control, feeling of hopelessness, blockage in the face of a situation that we cannot face, continuous negative thoughts.

The duration of the treatment will be determined. On one hand, what is the reason or the problem for which the person goes to psychological treatment: anxiety? Phobias? Emotional dissatisfaction without locating an exact cause? Difficulties in decision-making?

How long have you been living with this problem, and how it has evolved and taken root in aspects not only personal but also family, professional, etc.

We must understand that psychological treatment aims to produce changes and that making any change is a process that requires actions that transform aspects of our life, which sometimes costs a lot to modify.

Another aspect that influences the duration of treatment is the dynamics of clinical work itself. How much motivation is there in the process? How much involvement in the exercises proposed between sessions?

How much adjustment on the part of the professional to the techniques and treatments proven to be effective? Cognitive behavioral treatment is not a long-term therapy. On the contrary, it is considered an effective and brief treatment.

The important thing is that the treatment duration does not violate or detract from the planned objectives. The person always has clear and precise information on how and why psychological therapy is being developed at that rate.

So far, I have tried to answer what I consider the five most frequent questions about cognitive behavioral therapy, but there are others that I do not want to miss.

What if I am not sure about the orientation? What else will benefit me? How can I compare it with other options? What can I do to decide where to go?

The process of choosing a psychology center and professional is something especially difficult. It is common to reference someone close, which is usually an essential criterion in our choice, but is it enough?

Some steps before making this decision will be very useful for you:

1. **Get informed**. Decide what type of therapy you want to receive. Be interested in the type of treatments practiced in the centers where you consult, and ask for information about how the clinical procedure is in that therapy and if it is the best scientifically supported for your situation or personal problem. Question: What and how is it done? Is it the most effective? Why?

2. **Get up close**. When in doubt, have a first contact with the center and the professional you would work with. Before you take the step of starting treatment, go for an initial interview. In that contact, you can receive precious information about how the treatment will be and how you have felt talking to that person in whom you would place your trust.

3. **It requires the necessary health accreditations**. Choose a center with guarantees, where all psychologists have accreditation from the Official College of Psychologists; the center has all the pertinent permits for health activity; that at the administration level, it responds to all legal requirements: billing, data protection law, etc. All these guarantees are not only an expression of seriousness and rigor. They usually show well-organized and defined work systems, with protocols and control procedures that guarantee you a quality service.

4. **Look for confidence**. Choose with conviction where and with whom you want to work. Even before deciding, from the first contact, express your doubts, fears, and uncertainties about the process. See if the environment, the professional, and the type of treatment they offer you give you the conviction that you will need in the process.

5. **Seek safety**. It is legitimate to demand good treatment. But beyond this, make it easy! Choose professionals who have those qualities that you consider necessary. It's your choice! Intelligence, responsibility, good manners, commitment, tenacity, dedication, sensitivity, empathy, closeness, respect.

Emotional mind: adaptation and satisfaction

I'm going to ask you to think about situations that have made you feel bad. But first I want to ask you: do you consider yourself a person with good emotional skills?

Surely, in the last few weeks, you have been through some unpleasant experiences. Someone has not gone to an important appointment. You have not felt capable in the face of difficulty. Your child has reacted inappropriately with you.

You feel that your partner is less involved in your relationship, someone has told you something that you have felt unfair, they have rejected in a job interview, you feel displaced by some friends, you can't control something important that you want to change, someone tested positive for COVID-19…

What did you feel, with what intensity, how long did the discomfort caused by the situation persist? Did it scare you to feel bad? What did you do to stop feeling disgusted? What did you do to resolve the situation?

Take a moment before you start reading this section, write down the current situations that have affected you, and identify the following elements:

1. Situation (what happened).
2. Emotion (how you felt).
3. Thoughts (what ideas came up). Interpretation of the facts and the emotions that are felt.
4. Conduct (what did you do).

With this simple technique, you will observe your emotional states and identify your limitations or strengths when facing what happens to you in your day to day.

It will allow you to reflect on what aspects influence your emotional experiences, obtain information that you may have overlooked, and promote learning and adaptation.

The value of emotional competencies

Emotions play a fundamental role in the processes of adaptation to changes – desired or unforeseen. Also, in our activities' daily performance, in the learning processes, interpersonal interactions, and of course, in our well-being and health.

The confinement and health crisis has been a challenge for most people regarding the management of their emotions. We have implemented strategies of all kinds, physical and psychological, to promote a better adaptation and face uncertainty, reduce chronic interpersonal sources of gratification, promote pleasant emotions, despite difficulties, and devise ways to reduce or manage stress.

All of this has tested our emotional stamina. But it has also allowed us to become aware of our ability to mobilize resources aimed at managing complex emotions, organizing our priorities and needs, and trying to solve obstacles in these circumstances.

We have learned many things, we have had the opportunity to observe and know our strengths and abilities. The moments of introspection have most likely revealed aspects of our emotional management and coping that could be improved.

Life constantly puts us before a dilemma: lock ourselves and deepen in suffering, or adopt a resilient and learning approach, adapting to the situation in a productive way for our emotional well-being.

If we decide on the second option, we will need our emotional skills.

Emotional competencies can be defined as a set of knowledge, abilities, skills, and attitudes necessary to understand, express, and regulate emotional phenomena appropriately (p.22, Bisquerra, 2003).

Emotional competencies have become increasingly important as protective factors for personal and social health and well-being. They are considered predictors of success in academic life and at all levels of adult life (Ibarrola, 2014).

In the last two decades, they are increasingly valued and required in work and professional environments due to the constant technological transformations, which entail an effort to adapt, learn, and manage information.

Also, at the interpersonal level, emotional competencies are decisive. Society is increasingly complex and changing: multiculturalism, geographical mobility, globalization, multinationalism of personal relationships.

Emotional education in educational contexts is gaining relevance given the growing recognition of the role of emotions in teaching and learning processes and the positive impact on the development of people's potentialities and their psychological, physical, and social well-being.

What are emotional competencies? What are the main ones? Why are they so valuable? How are they learned and trained?

Emotions and affective states greatly influence many cognitive processes such as reasoning, attention, memory, and perception, fundamental in the processing of information.

Emotions can facilitate, distort, or inhibit central processes in the acquisition, assimilation, storage, and retrieval of information (De Aparicio, 2009).

Imagine that when you get home after a difficult day, where you are upset, angry, you see that the instructions you gave before leaving for work have not been followed.

Another day you would care less, but today: you see everything worse than it is (attention), you misinterpret what they tell you (information processing), and you remember – even if you don't want to – the time's something similar has happened to you (your memory is consistent with your state of mind).

But what would happen if you came happy, after a good day, and found yourself facing the same situation?

Emotions are psychophysiological reactions – cognitive, physiological, and behavioral responses – in response to external or internal situations, events, and demands, which predispose to action, through a rapid organization to face the experience.

For example, when we feel jealous – of a partner, co-workers, or friends – our body tenses, our pulse quickens, we activate our attention, and analyze events related to the situation. We act, we seek information, we value, we interpret. Not all people react in the same way to the same situation. Then there are different ways of dealing with the same situation and different emotional consequences.

Knowing how we react, what we feel, how we can regulate the different, more automatic emotional responses to improve our thinking and disposition to certain tasks or situations relevant to our well-being are emotional competencies that support emotional intelligence.

Thus, the result of doing things in an emotionally intelligent way would be, accepting jealousy as an emotion we can have, observing and understanding why it is, and acting to minimize jealousy, being realistic, and not damaging a good relationship due to unfounded assumptions.

Emotional competencies: the basis of emotional intelligence

The concept of emotional intelligence became popular with Daniel Goleman's "bestseller" (1995). However, it was Salovey and Mayer in 1990, who coined the term emotional intelligence and proposed a model based on different emotional abilities - which is one of the most consolidated today.

Emotional intelligence for these authors consists of managing our own emotions and those of others, discriminating between them, and using the information they provide us to guide our thinking and actions (Molero, Saiz & Esteban, 1998).

In other words, emotional intelligence would be the ability to process emotional information accurately and effectively: the ability to perceive, assimilate, understand, express, and regulate emotions, own and of others (Mayer and Salovey, 1997; Mayer, Caruso and Salovey 1999; 2001).

Thus, Goleman (1998) describes it as the ability to recognize one's feelings and those of others, motivate oneself, and manage one's emotionality and emotions in interpersonal relationships.

The principles or basic emotional competencies in adequate emotional intelligence are: self-knowledge, self-control, self- motivation, empathy, social skills, assertiveness, proactivity, and creativity in the way of facing and solving problems offers a comprehensive review of the different proposals regarding emotional competencies and proposes a model in which the different abilities are organized into five emotional competencies:

1. Emotional awareness

Ability to perceive, identify, and understand emotions in oneself or oneself and others through verbal and non-verbal expression.

- Facial expression.
- Voice tone.
- Body expressiveness.
- Adequate handling of emotional language.
- Empathy or understanding of the perspectives of others, get involved in their experiences.
- Read the situational and expression keys that have a degree of cultural consensus.

2. Emotional regulation

Ability to adequately handle emotions.

- Know the interactions between emotion, thought, and behavior.
- Expression of own emotions.
- Recognize and can regulate some feelings and emotions with a substantial impact on the behaviors they drive.
- Have skills to deal with unpleasant or uncomfortable emotions that favor the reduction in intensity, duration, and frequency of unpleasant emotions.
- In a complementary and vital way, it can self-generate and experience pleasant emotions consciously and voluntarily.

3. Emotional autonomy

This competence includes various characteristics and attitudes related to personal self-management: personal characteristics that allow external stimuli not to affect the person drastically, allowing them to be sensitive but with a certain capacity for self-protection.

- Possess positive self-esteem.
- Ability to self-motivate and get involved in various activities of life.
- Ability to take responsibility for decisions, to engage in healthy, safe, and ethical behaviors.
- Perception of emotional self-efficacy.
- Ability to resiliently face adverse situations.
- Interpersonal intelligence
- Ability to build and maintain good relationships with other people.
- Mastery of social skills, communication skills, and receptive listening.
- Ability to share emotions in a way appropriate to the relationship structure and context.
- Assertiveness.
- Prosocial and cooperative attitudes, respect, and acceptance of individual differences.
- Skills to prevent and solve problems or conflicts.

- Ability to face daily challenges and exceptional situations adaptively and responsibly, which allows us to organize life in a healthy and balanced way, contributing to experiencing satisfaction and well-being.
- The ability to set positive, achievable, and realistic goals.
- Decision-making in different areas of life.
- Seeking resources and support when necessary.
- The exercise of active, civic, responsible, critical, and committed citizenship.
- The ability to consciously enjoy well-being and try to transmit it to the people with whom you interact.

The organization in these emotional competencies will allow us to outline a framework or conceptual map for our self-knowledge, which allows us to recognize our strengths, what skills we are best at, and what our Achilles heel is.

Identifying our emotional competencies will undoubtedly be essential to begin a growth path and strengthening in the personal, professional, and social sphere.

There are five basic emotional competencies, and they are the basis of the so-called emotional intelligence. Each and every one of them is decisive for our well-being and happiness.

Sometimes we have misconceptions about emotions. Other times, we don't pay due attention and value to them. Our strategies may be inappropriate and ineffective or counterproductive in regulating the intensity or duration of what we feel.

Especially when experiencing intense emotions such as sadness, anxiety, anger, or fear, which can be perceived as uncontrolled and interfere with our normal social and psychological functioning.

Identifying, knowing, and improving our emotional competencies will help us manage our emotional world better, relate better with others, facilitate the achievement of our goals and objectives, and ultimately advance our well-being and personal growth.

Self-reflection: 3 questions about your emotional competencies

I propose three questions to start this interesting path towards your self-knowledge and expand the foundations of your emotional skills.

Use some everyday emotional reactions to increase your self-awareness:

- Identify what situation or event activated you. What was your emotional state like? How do you think you would react if you were cheerful, happy? What if you were mad or angry?
- Try to describe your thoughts and bodily sensations.
- If you thought differently, what would your emotional reaction be?

How do you change your negative emotions?

- Are you distracted, or do you think differently about what is affecting you?

- Do you focus on the positives?
- Are you trying to find solutions within your reach?
- Do you share your feelings with someone you trust?

Your communication with the people around you?

- Do they facilitate mutual understanding?
- Can they convey your emotions and opinions easily?
- Do they get you to understand other people's perspectives on disagreements?

Remember that this section's content is information. Even though it is scientific and rigorous and prepared by a team of experts, it has a formative, educational, or informative nature. It cannot be used or interpreted as a psychological or medical diagnosis. In health, specialists and accredited professionals are fundamental, who will always value each person's characteristics.

The global stigma around mental health

In recent times, more importance has been given to the disease of physical symptoms, but not so much to mental health, despite the WHO defining health as the complete state of physical, mental, and social well-being, and not only the absence of conditions or diseases.

We can go back to the end of the 1st century and the beginning of the 2nd century when the Roman author Juvenal wrote this Latin quote belonging to his satires "Mens sana in corpore sana." Something that we can interpret as the need for a healthy mind for a vitally important balance.

Canadian sociologist Erving Goffman is the author of a work entitled "Stigma," in which he defined stigma as the process in which the reaction of others spoils the "normal identity," recognizing the experience of mental illness as a form of stigma, it occurs in a wide variety of socio-political contexts in many parts of the world.

To address the stigma caused by mental illness, we must explain that it is a mental illness. Mental illness or disorder can be defined as an emotional, cognitive, or behavioral alteration in which basic psychological processes such as emotion, behavior, or learning are affected.

There are many mental diseases and disorders, including schizophrenia and psychotic disorders, mood disorders, anxiety disorders, dissociative disorders, personality disorders, adjustment disorders, bipolar disorder, somatoform disorders, and factitious disorders.

Mental illness is a great stigma in our society and especially in the developed world of the northern hemisphere. After an interview with a specialist in the field, and in which he dictates his diagnosis, the patient already lives with that stigma, the stigma of being seen differently from the rest of society, not fitting in, living socially isolated, and learn to live with a disease that often occurs chronically, with its consequent relapses and outbreaks.

Many people who have a mental disorder avoid talking about it to avoid social rejection. This link shows a video in which various patients tell about their experience with the disease and the difficulties they have had throughout his illness.

Most of society views these patients in derogatory terms, calling them 'crazy,' along with the belief that the mentally ill must be admitted to a psychiatric hospital.

According to the World Health Organization, one in four people will have a mental disorder in their lifetime, and by 2020 depression will be the second leading cause of disability in the world after coronary heart disease. Especially in the developed countries and the most robust economies of the northern hemisphere.

People with chronic mental illness have numerous rejection experiences, especially in the workplace, in social relationships, and in groups of friends: 44% claim to have had experiences of discrimination in the workplace, 43% in relationships with friends, and 32% with neighbors or their environment.

Some measures for the prevention of mental illnesses can be: regarding food, the consumption of vitamin B and DHA is recommended, which is a fatty acid that is part of Omega-3 and can be found in fish such as salmon or also in walnuts, almonds and peanuts; About exercise, it is recommended to carry out physical activities, thus allowing correct blood circulation in the cerebral vessels, optimizing mental function; In addition to exercise, intellectual activities such as reading and memory games are recommended.

I conclude with a phrase from the writer Ray Bradbury that says, "Madness is relative. It depends on who has whom locked in which cage". It is not a cause of infamy to suffer from a mental illness. The true infamy is not to be tolerant of those people who have a mental disorder. Usually, we talk about mental problems at a medical level: causes, symptoms, diagnoses, medications. Figures: how much of the population does it affect, what sex with the highest prevalence. However, this is never discussed, the taboo in our societies despite being something of such a high prevalence.

I doubt many people do not have close people with eating disorders, anxiety disorders, depression, etc. And it is very complicated because it is more, we have never been taught to learn to treat or help people with these types of problems, when what they need most is emotional support, to stop feeling like "strange creatures" and to feel integrated into a social circle.

On the other hand, the problems of depression are so much the order of the day and that everyone pretends not to know. Or if they know someone in this state, their contribution is to "dress up and paint yourself, and go for a walk," as if the person is unwell of their own free will.

Really, and unfortunately, today there is still this prejudice about people who we consider out of the "normal." Instead of listening to them and trying to help, we ignore them, turn our backs, mock and even make impediments so that they can develop a normal life. It is necessary to make known normally mental disorders, the people who suffer from them, and their internal struggle. With this, we will achieve its normalization in society. It is more important, in the health personnel who must support people with any type of physical or mental disorder contributing to their recovery. Still, we must apply it both to our work environment and in our daily lives.

Chapter 2: When the nights are blue and there's no meaning to it

We live in a culture that fosters wellness. We know what to eat, how many minutes to play sports and we spend hours staying relaxed to live better. But we have an Achilles heel: anxiety. According to the Anxiety and Depression Association of America, anxiety is the most common mental health problem, affecting more than 40 million adults across the United States.

However, anxiety is a natural protection mechanism, a psychological alert system that anticipates possible threats to avoid future problems. It is a state of restlessness, which **involves fear and stress at the same time when danger is not present**.

It's just an idea that springs up in your mind and creates the necessary stress to resolve your concerns before it's too late. Sometimes we have general anxiety that is not associated with any specific situation. It is nonspecific anxiety. Other times we know very well its origin: it is the specific one.

In both cases, it produces lightheadedness, nervousness, rapid heartbeat, sweating, tremors, choking, chest tightness, nausea, abdominal discomfort, dizziness, tingling (paresthesia), chills or flushing, fear of losing control, going crazy or dying, which produces isolation behaviors.

They are unpleasant enough sensations that we are often more afraid of anxiety itself than of the problem we are trying to solve: it is the fear of fear. If it is a normal emotion, why is it causing so much suffering and has it become an epidemic? Much of our education is based on being scared. According to Noam Chomsky, we live in the **"culture of fear"**, a term to define the process by which this feeling is disseminated through the media, political speeches, etc. and that influences people's behavior.

Also, we have developed a phobia of uncertainty. We have a mania for the control that, paraphrasing Giorgio Nardone, ends up leading us to the abyss of uncontrolled.

The stress response activates **adrenaline** and **norepinephrine first**. The former increases the heart, and respiratory rate oxygenates the blood and increases blood pressure. The latter increases the capacity for analysis and motor coordination.

Then, the secretion of cortisol is activated, which favors the creation of circulating glucose, ensuring food for the brain (neurons eat glucose). It favors the mobilization of fat deposits so that the muscles move towards flight or fight. The persistence of this hormone can be very harmful. The systems that can be damaged by the anxiety response and stress are:

- Immune (allergies)
- Genetic (modifications in chromosomes)
- Neurological (headaches, memory loss, dizziness)
- Digestive (abdominal pain, gastritis, diarrhea and constipation)
- Cardiovascular (tachycardia, hypertension, palpitations)
- Respiratory (increased respiratory rate, cough, rhinitis)
- Cutaneous (sweating, tingling, eczema, alopecia)
- Genitourinary (frequent urination, premature ejaculation, impotence and frigidity)

Can we die? No, directly, but it involves physical wear and tear that favors these diseases.

Guilt trips

What is the origin of this discomfort that makes anxiety so little functional? This question has only one answer: your thoughts, according to cognitive psychology.

These produce distortions when it comes to orienting yourself in the world. They are the glasses that each one wears to look at reality. Which is yours?

- Pessimism: Tendency to focus on the problem without being able to see the solutions
- Generalization: Thoughts are always generalized
- Negative thinking: The focus is on the negative aspects, and the positive aspects are forgotten or disqualified
- Catastrophism: Seeing the negative aspects of an excessive and exaggerated way
- Reading the thought: They think they know what others are thinking and their hidden cynical motives
- Guessing the future: Tendency to anticipate that things will go wrong
- Comparison: Measure yourself against others to always end up losing and feeling inferior
- Exaggeration: If someone makes a mistake once they become clumsy or if one thing goes wrong they are called a failure in all areas
- Guilt: Feeling that the unpleasant circumstances that happen are always related to oneself
- Perfectionism: Making demands on others, on yourself or on how things should be

The feeling of vulnerability

What makes us vulnerable to anxiety problems? Emotional education plays a vital role in managing these types of thoughts. Also, there is a hereditary predisposition to suffer it. If your family has a history of anxiety disorders, you will be 45% more likely to suffer from them.

They influence, in turn, personality traits. The factors that lead to threatening interpretations are neuroticism (tendency to experience situations as unpleasant); the high sensitivity; introversion or tendency to over-excitement.

According to a study conducted at the University of Cambridge, the incidence of anxiety disorders skyrockets among **people who have not reached 35 years** of **age**, many of them are still students, an activity that increases anxiety.

Women are twice as likely to suffer from these disorders associated with family factors. For men, they are linked to economic and labor aspects. Children and adolescents suffer them linked to their evolutionary development, in **babies of eight or nine months** due to the need for contact.

At one or two years, separation anxiety is common, especially from the mother. **Between three and six years** is the adaptation to school and, after seven, meet the expectations of adults.

In **adolescence,** concerns revolve around self-image, group acceptance, and the future. Children show anxiety with somatic disorders ("my gut hurts") and phobias (fear of wasps, for example) and adolescents with obsessive disorders.

Anxiety in the elderly manifests itself with the deterioration of intellectual faculties (executive function, processing speed, memory and attention). Specialized help is needed when:

- Alterations in the person's family, work and social life;
- There is a risk to the physical and psychological integrity of oneself or of others;
- When symptoms persist for at least a month;
- The concern about the possibility of having more crises appears.

The modification of limiting beliefs by functional thoughts and interoceptive exposure (exposure to feared bodily sensations) works. For example, if you fear tachycardia, go up and downstairs and then calm yourself with relaxation or breathing techniques.

With systematic desensitization, the feared situation is gradually faced, first in the company and driving the distance until facing it directly. "Fear is my most faithful companion, it has never tricked me into going with another," says Woody Allen. However, we cannot allow ourselves to be manipulated by limiting thoughts and learn to manage them so that they do not block our life.

What is it like to live with anxiety? The story of a man and a woman

My dear friend Thomas (33 years old) recalls that he does not remember her life without anxiety. At just five years old, he began to feel extreme anguish when he stayed with a caregiver and suffered a seizure.

"At first, I did not know how to name what was happening. I called it being afraid, but I was afraid of many things," he explains.

With the support of different psychologists, he learned what was happening to him: he had anxiety. Identifying it and coping with professional help have taught him that, although "he will always be an anxious person", he can learn to live with this emotion.

Anxiety is an innate adaptive capacity that is good; it prepares our body to face real danger and makes us able to flee from that danger more efficiently. However, as Thomas explains, when one suffers from an anxiety disorder "that fear seriously interferes in some important area of our life and becomes disabling."

If we look at the figures by gender, women who suffer from it almost double those of men. The symptoms of this disorder usually manifest in an alteration of the nervous system that produces hyperventilation, tachycardia and even dizziness.

According to the youth barometer of life and health, carried out by the Foundation for Help against Drug Addiction and the Mutua Madrileña Foundation, only half of the young people who feel symptoms of mental disorders go to a specialist.

Most cases of anxiety and depression begin in childhood and adolescence. By the time the patient demands care, more than ten years have passed, and they come to a consultation without having received any type of medical help.

However, with work and time, it can be minimized. From Thomas' experience, the key is that the person who suffers it "goes to a psychologist who teaches management and control strategies." Psychological treatment helps and does cure an anxiety disorder because it teaches you to manage it. And he adds: "More than controlling anxiety, you have to identify it, understand it and then regulate it."

I spoke to five more people who have learned to cope with their anxiety. Many of them began in childhood and adolescence, and all have been learning to handle it for years.

Helena García, 20 years old (Chicago)

"I have always suffered from anxiety. Since I was very little, I have felt nervous, very insecure, but I had not given it a name. I remember that in elementary school, I had problems to relate because I always thought about what they would think of me and that it generated a discomfort inside that gave me many problems.

"At the slightest feeling that something could go wrong I would start thinking about it and, after going all day at a thousand an hour in my head, I would go to bed and could not sleep. In high school, I remember three or four times that the next day I had an exam, and I could not go from the anxiety I had inside. I hadn't been able to stop crying all night, and I hadn't slept at all.

"Not sleeping started to become something that happened to me very often and my mother, who stayed up with me all night, told me one day that I couldn't go on like this and took me to the psychologist. By then, I was about 12 years old. Many people do not like to name their problems, but it helped me, because I knew something was wrong with me but not what it was. I saw that the source of my anxiety was my parents' relationship. As they were not well, I felt very lost, and that generated a lot of insecurities in me until I ended up exploding.

"When I was 14 years old, I had the occasional anxiety attack because everything came together: my parents ended up divorcing and it added to what I already had inside and to be in my teens. But at that age, I started with the medication and little by little. It got better. Some people believe that taking a pill is all right, but that is not the case. Medication without self-knowledge and without working on your emotions is useless. What I have improved since I started therapy until now is a world.

"Whenever I talk to people who have some kind of problem I tell them to go and ask for help. Although anxiety I don't think will go away (it is something that is part of my character) today I can say that you can control it and learn to live with it. But you always have to ask for help. It is useless if you keep it inside."

Caroline Armstrong, 27 years old (Denver)

"I started having generalized anxiety disorder when I was 20 years old. It was 2011, and I had just started a career in Gender Studies. Without really understanding the situation, I was walking down the street, and I felt sad and nervous. For example, on the subway, if I stopped between two stations, I would turn white and have a tachycardia. I felt paralyzed and even stopped riding on it. But then he couldn't put a name to something he didn't know."

Caroline began to have anxiety when she was 20 years old.

"My mother decided to take me to a psychologist when she saw me like this. While in consultation, I realized that I suffered from anxiety about a lot of things. I had a difficult adolescence, I am a very self-demanding person, and in high school, I felt that I had to comply with everything. She had to be the perfect partner, and if she wasn't, it frustrated me. I ended up paying for it with food, and I got really fat.

"In the end, anxiety is like the tip of the iceberg of what is happening to you. There are internal things that you have to solve. Going to therapy, I realized that I had the baggage of adolescence with complexes and that I felt insecure with myself.

"I spent four years with the psychologist; Four years that were hard, but also beautiful because they made me learn about my life, boost my self-esteem and feel more empowered. The person who started has nothing to do with who I am now. In your day to day affairs, you continue to have anxiety or that predisposition, but when you see it as a threat, you apply the techniques you have learned. "

Albert Miller II, 45 years old (New York)

"When I was 36 years old, I began to notice sensations in myself that I didn't know how to interpret. My father had died two years before, and that setback that I experienced I think made me more vulnerable. I spent a long time feeling dizzy, sleeping poorly and having the impression that everything I did at work was beyond me. I went to the emergency room for this feeling of dizziness (which made me even stop riding my bike) where they told me that I had nothing and that what I had to do was relax. But one day, I got up and exploded.

"I started crying like a child and told my wife that I felt unable to go to work. I took the step and took my first anxiety leave. I joined my job as Senior IT Manager after four months on the job and, after 11 years with the company, I was fired the same day I returned."

Albert realized that he was doing a job that he did not like.

"So I decided with my wife that the first three months of my son's life (who was born after the layoff) I would live with him at home. And those three months turned into three years. It was the perfect excuse to escape the subject and avoid the scenario where it had started: the world of work.

"I was interspersing other jobs, but for four and a half years it was all very intermittent because I kept giving up due to anxiety and they ended up firing me. But I found a psychologist who allowed me to understand how it affected me in my day to day life. It was here when I began to 'dominate' it, and little by little, it disappeared. After this, I realized that I was doing a job that I did not like, and after going against the current for so long, my body was manifesting it in this way.

"For a year and a half I have changed my life, I have stopped working as a computer scientist and have started volunteering in associations related to mental health. This has been somewhat therapeutic and, although I have sacrificed the purchasing power and advantages that my previous job offered me, the feeling I have is completely different. I have the reins of my life again. I wish the changes were not traumatic and with suffering involved, but in my case, it has been a change with which I have come out winning."

Pamela Wright Thompson, 33 years old (Los Angeles)

"I don't remember my life without anxiety. I started having it from a very young age. When I was five years old, I remember that I had a panic attack because my parents and my brothers went rafting to a river and I was left alone with a caretaker from the hotel where we were.

"At that time, I called it 'being afraid,' and I was afraid of many things. My parents found out and started taking me to the psychologist. Although she tells it like that, she was a happy girl, but she had many fears. I had a good time in high school, but when I got to college, everything started to get worse. I broke up with my partner. My family went through a process of seizure of our house… It was all very stressful.

"Also, a friend of mine committed suicide, and I started having obsessive thoughts that I was scared to kill myself too. I didn't want to, of course, but the very thought of it terrified me. From the anxiety that these thoughts produced in me, I even saw the crooked floor, and I found myself dizzy all the time. It was constant anxiety.

"I went back to the psychologist, and he said it was an 'impulse phobia' and that he was afraid of getting out of control. Those thoughts were intrusive, I didn't choose them, but they meant absolutely nothing: thinking about suicide did not mean that I was going to commit suicide, only that I had focused my stress on that idea.

"To this was added that in my environment, my anxiety was not well seen. People don't understand what anxiety entails, and this misunderstanding made me suffer much more than necessary. But with the psychologist, it went so well that I began to control it. I was 23 years old, and I started a radio master's degree, I started living alone.

"Little by little, I was coming out of that dark time of obsessions. I've never had a period of such anxiety like that again. Now I control it more, but it still affects me. I've always been anxious, and I realize it's one thing I'll always have. "

How to control anxiety?

Anxiety is a state of activation of the nervous system that is oriented towards the anticipation of danger, whether real or imagined. Being something so general, it has a physiological and a psychological aspect: in the first, there are phenomena such as tremors, sweating and acceleration of the pulse, and in the second there are phenomena such as the emotion of fear, the desire to avoid a stimulus aversive, and difficulties in controlling emotional responses to a situation.

Maintain regular routines

It is very important to be able to continue with the day to day routine, and that anxiety does not "gain ground". This means that the person must make an effort to maintain their activities and try not to avoid those situations that generate anxiety.

For example, if after the treatment you have managed to take the subway to go to work, even if it still generates a little anxiety, it is very important to continue practicing this situation to make the anxiety decrease

Play sports and doing exercise

Regular physical activity is advisable for almost everyone, and people with an anxiety disorder are no exception. Some scientific studies conclude that physical exercise (regular and moderate intensity) can help reduce and relieve anxiety symptoms.

Have good eating and sleeping habits

Maintaining proper eating and sleeping habits is essential to maintaining a healthy lifestyle. Sleeping for fewer hours than is recommended in a sustained way can cause irritability or stress, an aspect that can negatively affect anxiety symptoms.

Do not take stimulants in excess

The use of stimulants such as coffee, in high amounts and for long periods, can increase anxiety levels.

Avoid intoxicants

Some people with anxiety disorders use certain substances (such as alcohol or cannabis) to reduce the discomfort caused by some anxiety symptoms. However, doing this does not make the symptoms disappear in the medium / long term and increases the risk of problems related to substance abuse.

Be active on a social level

A good social circle that allows you to be active with friends can be a good tool to combat depressive symptoms (sadness or excessive apathy) that some people with anxiety disorders may have.

Share discomfort with the immediate environment

Some people can benefit from sharing their discomfort with those around them or with support groups. It is important to feel relieved, as well as for people around you to help identify the first symptoms of a relapse, for example.

Comply with the treatment

Following treatment, guidelines are important to combat anxiety symptoms. There are people with an anxiety disorder who may need to take medication for long periods. In these cases, the person may lose motivation, thinks about stopping the treatment or gets tired of some side effects. It is very important to express these doubts or reluctance to the health team to assess the best treatment options.

Enter depression

Depression does not always manifest it in the same way. Nor does it only imply a sad person who does not stop crying. There are many realities, and all of them deserve to be attended with the utmost professionalism and affection. Sufferers of depression are not always understood by society.

What is depression? Often this question has an easy answer when associating the word depression to the feeling of "being sad" or "having little desire to do anything".

Although in reality, these feelings are unpleasant. Sharing company with others suffering from depression would be just the tip of the iceberg of a disease that is increasingly present in our daily lives and with figures on the rise over the next few years.

Thus, a recent WHO estimate reveals that by 2020 of all diseases, depression will be the second most widespread in the world. As an additional characteristic that makes this disease especially dangerous and that is in the focus of mental health, is the presence of self-destructive behaviors in people who suffer from it.

Ultimately, to try to address depression, we cannot assume that this disease is only caused by "a handful of symptoms", such as feelings of sadness or dejection, not even as a syndrome (set of symptoms), such as sadness, anxiety, insomnia, etc.

It should be classified as a disorder, where this set of symptoms would be encompassed in a whole, which would affect the person who suffers from it in all its context, negatively influencing their family, partner, socially, in performance at work or study, in their health and the absence of daily activities in general.

What is the origin of depression?

Is there any cause that can explain its appearance? Much has been written about different factors or events that promote depression. Although these factors are not exclusive of other variables that may predispose to increase the appearance of the disease or prevent it from appearing, it is possible to speak of genetic or biochemical factors as a fundamental cause.

Regarding specific stressful situations that favor the appearance of depression, there are those situations of loss or grief, current or past traumatic situations and stressful factors in the life of this person, although as indicated above, the appearance or not of the disease, is the combination of such events with other biological and psychological factors,

Depression being, therefore a disorder, **how will it affect a person who suffers from it?** To understand the answer to this question, a support point must be established in the Beck (1973) model, which does not speak of a series of ad hoc characteristics, but the combination of the present symptoms, together with the evolution of these long-term symptoms, as well as the intensity of them.

Taking into account how these symptoms can evolve, a series of responses appear in people with the disorder:

- **Physiological/emotional responses:** Appearance of sadness, irritability, anxiety, sleep disturbances (excess or deficiency), loss of appetite, decreased sexual desire, the appearance of pain in the body's joints (knees, arms, jaw)
- **Cognitive responses**: Desire to escape, erroneous thoughts that increase the perception of disability of the person suffering from the disease, thoughts of guilt for not being able to get out of the situation, difficulty in making decisions, negative self-regard, negative world, denial of the future, attention difficulties, memory problems, suicidal ideas, passivity, difficulty in social relationships, dependence, loss of motivation and ability to enjoy and seek happiness.
- **Motor responses:** Difficulties falling asleep, waking up very early, agitation, psychomotor inhibition, crying.

These three responses are combined, forming a characteristic style of behavior in these people that are included in the famous "three A's."

- **Abulia:** Decreased interest and the ability to obtain pleasure in the activities that the person performs.
- **Apathy:** Feeling of lack of energy that leads these people to stop performing daily activities, because they find these activities especially heavy or tired.
- **Anhedonia:** Reduction of activities that the person suffering from the disorder found rewarding before the onset of the disease. The person stops going out with friends, attending family gatherings, doing sports or leisure activities in general, because they find their state of mind "stiff", not perceiving the happiness they used to find in such activities.

These styles of behavior make these people choose to be in bed or sitting in an armchair without the desire to actively assume any type of behavior, with feelings of hopelessness along with feelings of anxiety, and hyperactivity.

The depressed person sees their desire to continue with the usual activities altered, and the feeling of hopelessness immobilizes them to express their feelings, which ends up making it difficult for other members of a family or friends of this person to understand the seriousness of their state.

Depression is considered one of the most dangerous mental disorders that exist. As mentioned above, the functional state of the person who suffers from it is very deteriorated, but why consider dangerous a disorder that only affects the daily functioning of a person?

Indeed, if we let ourselves be carried away by the symptoms and signs of this disease, it does not seem that it is a serious disorder. However, let's analyze the self-destructive and hopeless thoughts of those who suffer it. It is not difficult for us to see the final solution that someone who spends many hours bedridden, analyzing all the characteristics of their life negatively, blaming themselves and not seeing a clear solution to their problems.

If, as stated in the previous point, depression is so serious, how is it possible that it is not stopped with useful prevention or intervention programs?

The answer at this point is clear, not because of financing problems or because there are no useful prevention programs, the answer to this question simply involves the behavior of the person who suffers from it. Thus, when it comes to diagnosing and treating the pathology, there are three types of possible cases:

- People who go to their primary care doctor, where they detect the depressive picture and an appropriate pharmacological and psychological treatment is established
- Those who go early to the primary care doctor, but depression is not detected. This can occur because the person does not want to admit that he or she has a mental disorder and derives attention to the organic symptoms, not paying attention to other signs or mental processes that the patient decides to omit or the doctor does not ask.
- Finally, those people who decide not to go to the primary care doctor, making their disorder chronic.

Which of these three types of cases occurs most often?

The first case, although it would be the most appropriate, is the least frequent. The second of the three cases, although present, is no longer so present, since there are currently very competent programs in the global healthcare system that have improved the diagnosis of the disease.

As for the last case, unfortunately, it is the most frequent. Since people with depression, omit from their family and friends the seriousness of their thoughts or feelings, leaving only their motor behavior evident, passing their friends or family to perceive them as a "lazy", "crybaby" or "exaggerated" person who spends all day lying down without doing anything, lamenting his sadness, in such a way that they avoid going to a specialist.

This increases the chances of the disorder to manifest further. And therefore, the severity and probability of self-injurious behaviors, the most serious being suicide. According to WHO data, a person with depression is 30 times more likely to threaten his life than any other person.

This inability to request help has become the most urgent problem in public health, since in most cases, when people with depression go to primary care, they do so because other symptoms that afflict these people are observed, in greater case anxiety or panic attacks.

As if that were not enough, it is currently estimated that this mood disorder is among the most prevalent psychiatric conditions. Thus epidemiological data suggest that 17% of the population reported having experienced depression at some point in their life; that is, at least once a day, primary care physicians treat a person with depression.

If this disorder has the World Health Organization in check, **what are the expectations for treatment or cure?**

Undoubtedly, drug treatment with antidepressants is the most widely used and fundamental treatment to tackle the problem in the short-medium term. However, it has been proven that in the long term, the possibility that the disorder may appear is greater.

Then a combined treatment is exercised with some type of psychological therapy.

Although cognitive-behavioral therapy is the one that has been used the most for its effectiveness and many years of experience, as well as the research behind it, new therapies are currently appearing that are showing even better results. These are the third generation behavioral therapy or ACT, Cognitive-Analytical therapy and EMDR therapy.

In any case, it is the combined pharmacological and psychological treatment that has the best results not only in the first phases of treatment but also in the prevention of relapses.

The reasons and symptoms are different according to gender and are linked to social constructions.

You cannot cry because crying does not come from you. Sometimes you don't want to talk because you don't know what to say. This is how Rodrigo Vera, a 28-year-old communication specialist, defines depression. For him, to suffer, it is to carry inside the biggest hole.

Depression is a mental disorder that is different from the usual mood swings. Depressive episodes can be classified as mild, moderate or severe. At least one in five people will have a depressive episode before reaching the age of 75.

Rodrigo suffers from chronic depression. However, it is estimated that the number could be higher due to how complex it is to identify the disorder. Although in many cases depression is described as a "deep nostalgic mood", he speaks of life in depression as "unpleasant", like a void that is not filled with music, food, colors, reading or loved ones.

"I identify myself among people who appear to be fine, but who suddenly enter into crises that seem to come out of nowhere. And on other occasions I don't identify with any of the symptoms that you see on the subway posters about depression and suicides," Rodrigo explains in one of our exclusive conversations for this chapter.

Unlike sadness, depression is a condition that has physical and cognitive symptoms. The two main ones are feeling sad most days of the week with a duration of at least two weeks and anhedonia, which is the loss of will, desire, interest or pleasure for things that previously did cause it.

There are physical symptoms such as insomnia or sleeping too much, increased or decreased appetite, memory problems or to maintain long periods of attention, which are related to forgetfulness, confusion and poor school or work performance.

Having ups and downs in a society like the current one is the norm, it would be strange if we didn't have them. However, it emphasizes the importance of not confusing between transitory states, which all people go through, and the diagnosis of depression.

Depression in women

"One of the problems I had with my mother was getting her to accept that something was wrong with me. For her, going to the psychologist was an exaggeration, a way of seeking care. And if we were talking about a psychiatrist, even worse," says 26-year-old Teresa Robles.

She wants both her mother and her friends to understand that feeling like this is not her decision and that having depression does not mean "being sad all the time". For Tere, living with depression has been a journey in which she has understood that there is nothing wrong with feeling this way, but that at the same time it is something to fight to avoid being a prisoner of the disease.

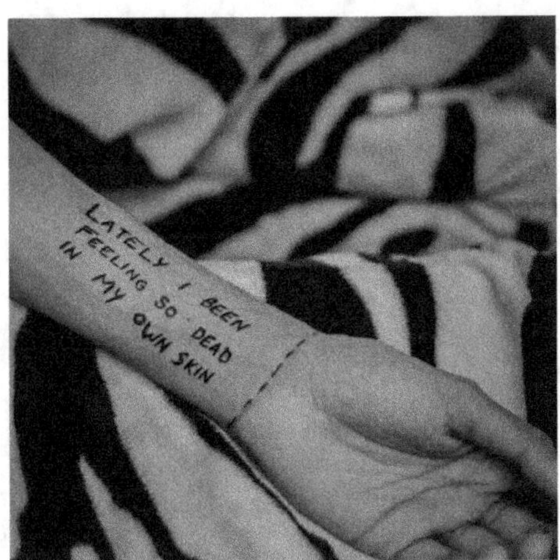

Clara Fleiz Bautista, from the "Ramón de la Fuente Muñiz" National Institute of Psychiatry, explains that for every two women with depression, one man suffers from it. This prevalence of the disorder is mainly due to gender stereotypes that generate anguish or tension for women.

Frequently, the mandates of motherhood, femininity related to aesthetics and gender violence, are associated with the depression experienced by women, the researcher Lucía Ciccia also agrees. "The symptoms to which depression is associated are linked to feelings, and that is something that is deeply associated with the feminine".

According to the specialist, the fact that the symptoms are "feminized" is because women express sadness more easily with crying or seeking medical attention. At the same time, men tend to express depression through irritability or anger.

The psychologist by the UAM, specialized in care for women survivors of gender violence, Martha Viniegra, estimates that depression in women is diagnosed three times more frequently than in men.

"Masculinity prevents you from going to the doctor until there is a crisis. Men are educated to seek success, be assertive and self-confident, but women are not".

On the other hand, men register a greater consumption of substances such as alcohol or drugs, often to "mask a psychiatric problem such as depression or anxiety and to substitute medical attention." Another revealing fact is that unsuccessful suicide attempts are more common in women, while men do tend to commit suicide.

When Tere was prescribed medications to treat the depression and anxiety that she was diagnosed with, her mother objected to her taking them, not believing what was happening to her and thinking that she was going to become dependent on them.

Adults with depressive episodes or with chronic depression usually undergo treatment that lasts 9 to 12 months, but it does not apply to all types of depression.

A parameter for prescribing medications to a person with severe depression is when they have a complete loss of sleep or, on the contrary, they sleep for days. Besides, they are absent from work or school and do not see their loved ones as often as before.

Patients often believe that they will not be well again without the help of medications or that they will need other treatments to feel well. It is as if the person with diabetes says he cannot depend on his medicine. It is a deficiency that the body has and must be resolved with some treatment or therapy.

The specialist likes the comparison between diabetes and depression, because just as the diabetic patient is not only treated with medication, those with depression must also do the "diet and exercise" that diabetic patients would do. In this case, they are psychotherapies.

Talk about depression

Many people avoid talking about depression or any mental health topic because they are topics that "carry a negative charge, compared to success, that is painted with a smile." The world abounds with examples of people who are considered successful (with work, family and pleasures) and despite that feel sad.

In the world, 300 million people suffer from depression, a figure equivalent to the entire population of Indonesia. Despite being such a common disease, there are taboos around it that must be eliminated to face it as the serious public health problem that it is.

"I think that the people closest to me think that my problem is not a problem and that is something dangerous because when I fall into those states of sadness, I feel deeply alone and responsible. For me, that is the biggest dilemma of depression," shared Rodrigo.

Dr Lucía Ciccia defines depression as a social epidemic that does not have viral contagion but feeds on the ease with which it is diagnosed, and antidepressants are presented, instead of pointing out the structural factors that generate this health problem.

"Generating social conditions in which you can move in a way that makes you feel better is much more difficult than taking a pill. Although a pill is necessary as a palliative in extreme cases, it should not be the easy medicine or the solution", says the CIEG researcher.

Movies that accurately depict mental illnesses

Taboos surround mental illnesses, and it is difficult to understand the situation of the people who suffer from them. Currently, we live in a world where culture is influenced by film and television. A great option to help society understand, empathize and understand.

Any movie offers a psychological reading of its characters and their way of thinking. It is very important to find characters with whom we feel identified. For this reason, it is just as important that people who suffer from some type of mental illness or those who care for a dependent person feel identified with certain cinematographic characters.

Personality disorders, schizophrenia, Alzheimer's and many more pathologies are reflected in the cinema. However, most of the time, the visibility they give to mental illnesses is usually unrealistic and even dangerous.

The mentally ill are often depicted as delusional murderers or villains; this is a gross misrepresentation of reality. For this reason, I have numbered the films that realistically present mental illnesses, to understand the people who suffer from these mental illnesses.

The best mental illness movies to understand:

Always Alice (2014)

It is a film that tries to bring us closer to the feelings of those who have Alzheimer's and their families.

Alice is proud of the life that has taken her so much effort to build. At 50, she is a professor of psychology at Harvard and a world-renowned linguist expert, with three grown children and a successful husband.

One day, she begins to feel disoriented, and a tragic diagnosis changes her entire life, influencing her relationships with her family and with the entire world. Alzheimer's has come to mind.

Love and other drugs (2011)

Maggie is a girl who will not allow anything or anyone to tie her up in her day to day life. Everything changes when you find your ideal partner. Jamie is an attractive 30-year-old man who does not hesitate to use his charm on girls and who lives in the ambitious world of pharmaceutical sales.

What at first starts as a relationship based on sex and ease, ends up becoming a relationship full of obstacles. Jaime's great dedication to his work is a great obstacle, but the worst is the secret that Maggie keeps; suffers from a degenerative disease, Parkinson's.

Melancholy (2011)

This film paints a very realistic picture of how the world collapses every day for people who suffer from depression, although the next day they may see everything better.

Justine sabotages her wedding night and falls into an almost catatonic depression. You cannot bathe or eat without having an ash taste in your mouth. Each member of her family represents a trait of humanity that contributes to Justine's state of mind.

Black Swan (2010)

Black Swan is based on metaphor to achieve perfection, whatever the price to achieve it.

Nina, a brilliant dancer from New York, lives completely absorbed by dance. She has an eating disorder as well as chronic hallucinations.

Many professionals in the world of dance suffer from eating disorders. The anorexia nervosa is one of the most common eating disorders and is considered the deadliest mental illness today.

The Machinist (2004)

The driver shows a very real vision of what it is like to suffer from chronic insomnia.

The protagonist of this film, Trevor, suffers from an extreme case of insomnia. This affects your day-to-day life and brings you numerous problems.

Trevor begins to hallucinate while at work and leaves his colleagues in dangerous situations without realizing it. For this, they blame him for several incidents and make his life impossible.

He ends up paranoid, fighting with everyone and constantly seeing hallucinations. *Will he be able to recover?*

Noa's Diary (2004)

The film is based on a love story told through Noa's diary, which he reads to his wife continuously. He hopes that his wife will remember what she had experienced with him and so he can enjoy a few seconds of lucidity with his wife since she has Alzheimer's.

Big Fish (2003)

A nice story of a boy with his father. William does not have a good relationship with his father Albert. Still, after learning that he is terminally ill, he returns to his side: Albert has a schizotypal personality disorder and spends the day telling his endless stories from his youth.

On this occasion, William will try to find out things that will allow him to know his father better. To do this, you must distinguish between reality and fantasy.

A Wonderful Mind (2001)

It is a biographical drama of the famous mathematician John Nah. The story is based on John's life, as he slowly develops paranoid schizophrenia.

The film gives an insight into how to learn to live with schizophrenia and fight for all your dreams despite it.

Memento (2000)

"Memento" is a confusing and entertaining movie at the same time. It shows us two different versions of the same scene throughout the movie. In black and white, in color and with different timelines. This is for the public to put themselves in the shoes of Leonard, a character suffering from anterograde amnesia.

Anterograde amnesia is a memory disorder that prevents a person from creating new memories after the event that caused dementia.

Fight Club (1999)

In *"Fight Club"* we have two main characters: an unnamed narrator and Tyler.

Tyler is a pimp who makes soap; the narrator is dissatisfied with his life who suffers from a multiple personality disorder. The narrator turns into Tyler to make up for his lack of power and masculinity. It portrays the disease very well and is a legitimate representation of how intense this disorder can be.

Why therapy?

Although society evolves and accepts new cultures, new fashions, and new diseases, mental disorders remain an indecent subject; Many times the fact of attending a psychological consultation is strange for others, for which the acceptance of a mental illness for those who suffer from it, becomes much more complex. Not to mention that the suffering produces a cognitive deterioration reflected in distorted thoughts and irrational ideas, which become the daily lives of patients, taking away the tranquility of them and those around them.

In this sense, the vast majority of people who are diagnosed with a mental illness, their therapy begins with taking pharmacological medications (psychiatry), to stabilize the person from their altered state of consciousness; However, cognitive-behavioral therapy has proven to be an indispensable tool for obtaining more effective prognoses in treatments.

On the other hand, the diagnosis of a mental disorder includes significant changes in the life of the person suffering from it and of those around him, the transformations can range from eating behavior to creating a new social circle, forcing the patient to modify many areas of your life.

In this vein, it becomes clear that the impact of the diagnosis of any physical and mental illness generates various questions in the patient, such as: where does the disease come from? Why does it give? Cure? Why me? Which on occasions, tend to be answered inadequately or simply not answered, which causes patients who drop out of the treatments and constant relapses.

Among the treatments available for those who suffer from some type of mental disorder, psychoactive drugs and psychotherapy are considered, which have shown similar efficacy if we stick to the mere reduction of symptoms.

However, psychiatry has sometimes fallen short as a single treatment, which has promoted psychotherapy as a complement to the efficiency of the processes, is as well as recently the World Psychiatry magazine, one of the most renowned psychiatric publications at an international level, has shown the effectiveness of the interventions psychological disorders in the treatment of serious mental disorders, in the absence of new drugs that act effectively.

However, it continues to seem like a second option.

According to the Diagnostic and Statistical Manual (DSM) in its different versions, it conceptualizes mental disorder as "a syndrome or a behavioral or psychological pattern of clinical significance, which appears associated with discomfort, a disability or a significantly increased risk of dying or of suffering pain, disability or loss of freedom."

This manual makes categorization of types of mental disorders, which demand different methods and patient care, either with pharmacological and psychological treatments; the latter, the psychological model that best adapts to the DSM is the cognitive one (psychotherapy cognitive), which is based on the diagnostic criteria of this manual and proposes that "all mental disturbances have in COMMON a distortion of thought, which influences the mood and behavior of patients".

Thus, one of the treatments for mental disorders is psychotherapy, which is presented as a procedure where a professional in psychology uses techniques to help a person overcome their psychological difficulties, to achieve psychological well-being and the adaptation of the subject; in this, there are several approaches and intervention techniques, which allow the patient the most appropriate choice of his therapist.

In the case of psychotherapeutic support in the diagnosis of a mental illness, cognitive-behavioral therapy is presented as one of the first choice treatments, based on the principles, mechanisms and processes that govern abnormal behavior provided by other scientific disciplines of psychology, such as psychopathology, learning psychology, and cognitive psychology.

About the above, in 1998 the American Psychological Association, to evaluate the efficacy of psychological treatments, established the following criteria for measuring the effectiveness of therapies, if: "their efficacy is empirically supported by results of at least two intergroup experimental studies or 10 SINGLE-case experimental studies, which demonstrate that said therapy is superior to drug treatment, a psychological placebo or another alternative psychological treatment, or that it is equivalent to a well-established treatment ".

This is how this therapeutic approach is focused on problems and difficulties of the here and now, that is, it works directly on the irrational and the distorted in mental illness as its maintenance factors; for this, the main objective is the solution of the patient's problems, through behavioral, cognitive and emotional change. One of the key characteristics is that it lies in the subjective and behavioral connections of the beliefs, feelings and actions of the patient, regardless of whether these beliefs are based on reality.

Besides, these are two models with a wide research trajectory: cognitive and behavioral; the first focuses on the identification of mental schemes and processes, with which the patient interprets and gives a meaning about himself and the world; the second is based on external behavior, and the basic processes of learning; The union of these two approaches aims to modify the way people think, through strategies investigated in advance with case studies.

Some of the strategies are systematic desensitization, Ellis's rational emotional-behavioral therapy, Beck's cognitive therapy, among others. Mixed procedures, where work is done on the cognitive, affective aspect and behavioral, are the best since they encompass the whole person".

Likewise, what cognitive-behavioral psychotherapy seeks in the treatment of mental disorders is for the patient to show his interpretations about his disease, understand it and, above all, accept it, helping him to define goals and teaching him to apply techniques psychological that contribute to reducing the discomfort associated with the disorder.

It is important to note that in most medical treatments for mental illnesses, pharmacology plays a fundamental role for the stability and proper functioning of the subject, however, not all people have the ability to transform their lives and accept a disease.

But then, what happens if the medications do not clarify the thoughts, the way of seeing the world and the issues that patients present? It is there where the biological factor ceases to be the main one, and other factors such as sociocultural and psychological are included.

Psychotherapy is charged with power and becomes necessary in this process, to create awareness of the disease, for adherence to pharmacology, knowledge of its symptoms, early arrest of episodes, to help a patient to distinguish and recognize what affects him, encourage responsibility, self-care, the ability to choose and decide, evaluating and assuming the consequences that this implies.

Additionally, cognitive-behavioral psychotherapy offers psychoeducation for the families or caregivers of the patient, training them on the diagnosis and providing them with the tools to understand and manage the person who suffers from it. Also, they are given a guide on what factors can improve or worsen the prognosis, reducing the burden and stress of the family, achieving greater emotional stability.

Psychoeducational programs for family members aimed at increasing knowledge about mental illness and changing attitudes are USEFUL within the scope of family intervention, in reducing the risk of relapse in patients.

On the other hand, it is important for the effectiveness of the treatment, that between the therapist and the patient, a level of trust (rapport) is achieved that allows them to establish a transparent conversation, where the patient freely expresses their thoughts, without fear of feeling judged or rejected.

This connection enables the therapist to assume a leading role in the life and recovery of the person suffering from the diagnosis, "supported by the certainty that he has a knowledge and an attitude to put them in favor of the well-being of his patient, and as a consequence, the patient assumes a submissive and waiting position in front of the cure. For all that has been said, it is important to analyze the benefits that psychotherapy can have in the lives of patients, prioritizing it as a comprehensive treatment for them; However, the diagnosis of mental illnesses can be similar to a dental problem.

It can suffer like a toothache due to cavities, and this causes the person to attend their dentist, who immediately performs an oral cleaning, stabilizing the pain, also gives a series of recommendations, such as brushing their teeth three times a day and for greater care and efficiency the use of dental floss. Many patients are left with the first recommendation as it is the most used, and dental floss takes a back seat.

Similarly, in the diagnosis of mental disorders, they are generally made when the patient goes into crisis, he goes to a psychiatrist, who, like the dentist, tries to reduce the symptoms with medications, achieving mental stability immediately.

 However, the psychiatrist makes a series of recommendations, among which is attendance at psychotherapy and support groups, which allow them to educate themselves about the disease; recommendation that is evaded by the patient, who, for the most part, prioritize the use only of drugs and omits attendance at psychotherapy, which produces less effective treatments.

It is necessary to increase the effective perspective compared to psychotherapy, because only a small proportion of patients suffering from mental disorders receive therapeutic support, even though this is valid and efficient, and can be used much more generalized. Thus, it is of great importance to encourage in the field of mental health, among medical professionals, psychiatrists and psychologists, that from their exercise, the treatment of disorders is complemented with psychotherapy, as a priority tool in education, control and acceptance of the patient in his diagnosis. So that the results are more successful and social, personal, emotional and physical benefits can be obtained that allow you to have a life with greater well-being.

Chapter 3: The Global Crisis of Mental Health

Mental health is described as a state of well-being in which people are conscious of their skills. It has to do with encouraging well-being, preventing mental illnesses and treating and rehabilitating individuals affected by these conditions.

Depression and anxiety disorders are prevalent mental health conditions that influence the ability to function and productivity. More than 300 million people, recognized as one of the major causes of disability, suffer from depression. More than 260 million people in the world have anxiety disorders at the same time.

In Latin America, the prevalence of psychiatric and neurological disorders over 12 months (or the number of cases during this period ranges between 18.7 and 24.2 percent; that of anxiety disorders, between 9.3 and 16.1 percent; that of affective disorders, between 7.0 and 8.7 percent; and that of psychoactive drug use disorders, between 3.6 percent and 5.3 percent.

According to the WHO Mental Health Action Plan, persons with major depression or schizophrenia are 40 to 60 percent more likely than the general population to die prematurely because of physical health conditions that are often not treated (e.g. cancers, cardiovascular disease, diabetes, and HIV infection) and suicide.

Equally wide are the economic effects of mental disorders such as depression or others. A World Economic Forum report estimated that between 2011 and 2030, the total global effects of mental illness in terms of economic losses would be $16.3 billion.

A brief history of mental illnesses

1906: At the XXXVII Southwest German Psychiatric Conference, the pathologist and psychiatrist Alois Alzheimer presented a specific cerebral cortex disease.

1949: Mental Health America launches efforts in the United States to commemorate Mental Health Month in May.

1996: publication of the work on the global burden of mental illness by the WHO and the Institute for Health Measurement and Evaluation.

2011: Publication by the WHO of the Intervention Guide for mental, neurological, and substance use disorders.

2012: The 65th World Health Assembly adopted resolution WHA65.4 on the global burden of mental disorders and the need for a comprehensive and coordinated response by the health and social sectors of the countries

2013: The World Health Assembly approved a comprehensive plan of action on mental health for 2013-2020.

2017: The World Health Assembly endorsed the Global Plan of Action on the Public Health Response to Dementia 2017-2025.

It is difficult to find a concept so diffuse and so used at the same time as that of mental health. The notion of mental health refers to a state or condition of the individual, to a field – conceptual and practical – within public health, to a series of psychiatric pathologies and psychosocial problems, even to a set of health and social initiatives.

Since the end of the Second World War and until today, mental health has acquired an extraordinary role, both at an academic and political level and in the daily life of Western societies. In 1946, the *Mental Health Association* was founded in London and, two years later, the First International Congress on Mental Health was held in the same city.

The World Health Organization, since its origins in 1948, has a Mental Health section. And in 1949, the *National Institute of Mental Health was created in the USA.* This reflects the interest in the great world powers' subject for decades, which, far from diminishing, grows every day.

It is not an exaggeration to say that we are experiencing a true mental health boom, although we do not always know what we are talking about.

In 1950, a WHO expert committee presented the first definition of mental health, clearly influenced by dynamic psychiatry. The three criteria proposed to define a mentally healthy person are:

- Achieving a satisfactory synthesis of one's instincts, potentially conflictive
- Establishing and maintaining harmonious relationships with others
- The possibility of modifying the physical and social environment.

It should be noted that we are in the difficult post-war years and that the term that is most repeated in this definition is "harmony." Shortly after, in 1958, the social psychologist Marie Jahoda published her famous systematization of positive mental health in the USA – created at the behest of the *Joint*

Commission on Mental Illness and Health –, which has been widely disseminated, simplified, and which undoubtedly constitutes the most obvious reference of all subsequent definitions.

The criteria proposed by Jahoda are:

- Realistic self-concept, identity, and self-esteem,
- Search for growth and self-actualization
- Integration of oneself and the different experiences,
- Autonomy,
- Objective perception of the reality
- Mastery of the environment: adaptation and success to achieve goals

For decades, we have bodies of the highest level in charge of mental health, and with more or less official definitions. However, these descriptions, in addition to not being without criticism, are outweighed by the daily use of the notion of mental health.

And it is actually: "mental health is presented as a generic object, under which a dispersed set of discourses and practices on mental disorders, psychosocial problems, and well-being are sheltered"; discourses and practices that "obey the rationalities of the different approaches to health and disease in the field of public health, philosophy, psychology, anthropology, psychiatry, among others, and therefore, mental health conceptions depend on these approaches and the ideologies that underlie them" (Restrepo & Jaramillo: 2012, p. 203).

It is difficult to understand that kind of kaleidoscope that both mental health-oriented practices and the definitions of mental health constitute without delving into the disciplines and discourses that have contributed to creating this field.

Psychiatry, the different psychotherapies, and movements critical to psychological and psychiatric clinics, such as antipsychiatry, community psychology, and other movements closer to social medicine and even to political action.

In general, both in academic texts, public plans and policies, and health services, the expression "psychiatry and mental health" is used. The use of the conjunction indicates that we should not confuse both terms, fields, or disciplines, that psychiatry and mental health are two issues that go together, but at the same time, that they are different.

And it is not that psychiatry is the means and mental health is the end. Cardiology services, for example, are not designated as "cardiology and cardiovascular health." This seems to be due rather to three reasons:

- The neuropsychiatric nature of the mental hygiene movement (precursor of mental health organizations and actions).
- Social matters are included within mental health problems that could hardly be considered a psychiatric pathology in a strict sense.
- The strong presence of professionals who do not come from a biomedical matrix in mental health.

Due to its proximity to public health, there is a tendency to think about promotional and preventive actions, which necessarily leads to going outside the health area. Taking the focus off patients to look towards the environment is called "the community."

However, that is not the case when generating plans, programs, allocating resources, calculating costs, etc. Mental health appears to be reduced to a series of disorders, termed "mental and behavioral." Mental health services, units, or departments usually delimit their range of action in a rather conventional way, based on a list of disorders that would be their specialty.

Rather a fuzzy boundary.

Not many years ago, epilepsies crossed the frontier of psychiatry towards neurology. And many voices argue that psychiatry should assume that it is nothing but a subspecialty of neurology, since, strictly speaking, there would be no mental disorders, as it would be brain dysfunctions, that is, neurological problems (Baker & Menken: 2001).

The coherence of this point of view must be recognized. While it may seem politically incorrect to deny mental health, in practice, most psychiatrists and not a few psychologists function as if this were the case. And it shouldn't be surprising; it is a logical derivation of modern medicine's path and the aspirations of leading figures in psychiatry history, such as Kahlbaum, Kraepelin, or Schneider.

Furthermore, it would be in continuity with Western medicine, in its Hippocratic-Galenic aspect. The discussion of whether the sick soul or only the body has that possibility, whether there are moral illnesses or are the effects of the corruption of the body, is very old.

This is also how, on the other frontier, some see the opening of a vast field of existential and social problems as the characteristic of psychiatry: "Psychiatrists are called upon to treat problems that the medical-industrial complex hardly responds to. Such problems – paradoxically – constitute the most 'novel' of the psychiatric in the health system" (Lolas: 2008, p. 97).

Beyond how psychiatry will resolve its internal differences, it is impossible to ignore the psychiatric imprint in any approach that is made today to mental health. As a branch of medicine, although it is rather implicitly, psychiatric practice equates health and normality, and normality to functionality.

For this reason, it is not surprising that for a long time, psychometrics has been the main source of links between psychologists and psychiatrists. Psychometric tests are parallel to laboratory tests in physical medicine, assuming that the mind is just another organ, invisible, but that it has its physiology. Therefore, its own rules.

Likewise, this allows us to understand the facility for psychiatrists to implement interventions to modify the environment: suggesting job changes, indicating vacations, promoting marital separations, etc. In a physiological conception of mental health, it is necessary to ensure that the organism is not over-demanded by the environment's demands.

Definitions that point to "internal balance" are, at heart, physiological. It should be remembered that physiology imposed the ideal of homeostasis, self-regulation, a proverb of health, and a guarantee of individual autonomy.

From this physiological approach also come all definitions of mental health that appeal to "functioning"; for example, when the WHO indicates that the positive perspective conceives mental health as the *optimal state of functioning*. Therefore, aspires to promote the qualities of the human being and facilitate their maximum potential development.

The key, or rather, what could make a difference within this perspective, is how mechanistic or without the subject a physiological conception of health can become. On the other hand, what would be the expected effects of the brain's balance or good functioning?

Sigmund Freud

At the same time, medicine was definitively becoming applied biology, and psychiatry left behind the moral treatment and any link with philosophy – succumbing to the pessimism of the Theory of Degeneration. A group of neurologists, faced with the mysteries of the so-called "neuroses," in particular hysteria, opted for psychogenesis and word treatments.

These are known works of Charcot, Janet, Breuer, and of course, Freud. And although the modern term psychotherapy is the creation of JH Bernheim – who intended the legitimate and conscious use of suggestion in the cure – it is only with psychoanalysis that psychotherapeutic practice begins to acquire its own and recognized status and logic.

Because?

What differentiates Freud from his predecessors is that he elaborates not only on an explanation and treatment for hysterical symptoms but general psychology, whose two fundamental pillars are the notion of the unconscious and the drive.

As the unconscious and the drive are part of the human condition, the gap between healthy and sick becomes blurred, and psychotherapy is no longer an exclusive offer for those who have a diagnosis.

On the other hand, while doctors discard the patient's word in search of objective signs, Freud insists on a clinic of listening, which puts the symptom and its interpretation at the center of the medical act.

This is because the symptoms would be speech, messages, which refer to unconscious desires for the subject. Desires that ultimately lead to an impossible search, while total satisfaction is forbidden for the human being.

If in the beginning, mental health for Freud is in the possibility of making the unconscious conscious, which means subjecting the empire of reason to the fancies of passions ignored for the subject. Therefore, the paradoxical condition of the human being gives mental disorders an existential status.

Freud argues that the psychoanalytic cure offers are only better arrangements. Better in what way? In the possibility of enjoying and producing, loving, and working. This is how the mental health of an individual is known.

Freud is not alien to a physiological conception of health, insofar as he thinks of the mind as an "apparatus," with subsystems, instances, and functions. For the same reason, the difference between health and pathology would be somewhat quantitative.

But what psychoanalytic cure is about? In his late work, it is increasingly about knowing how to live, about having the fortitude and wisdom to take charge of being alive, a life that Freud was far from a paradise.

In other words, the therapeutic objective is closer to an ethical horizon, in the classic sense of the term, to a kind of knowing how to do with one's own life. So much so that those collaborators who later departed from Freud and created their psychotherapeutic currents, such as A. Adler, CG Jung,

Meanwhile, in the United States, the rise of the behaviorist movement made little relevance for psychologists and the psychological clinic, the very notion of mental health. The mind cannot be studied scientifically, nor does it seem necessary when explaining human behavior.

Behaviorism questions the concept of mental illness as an entity and maintains that what exists are maladaptive behaviors. That turn had an enormous impact on the psychological clinic, and therefore, on conceiving mental health.

Darwinism

It is known that American Academic Psychology, from functionalism onwards, including Psychoanalytic Psychology of the Ego and Cognitive Psychology, is strongly influenced by Darwin's ideas.

In this sense, you cannot talk about the individual's health without looking at the environment since health is measured in its ability to adapt to it. Normality aspiration loses weight, and health becomes rather synonymous with adaptation. Whether it is behaviors, the self, or cognitive schemas and processes, the north of all mental health treatment is to make the corresponding adjustments and corrections based on a better adaptation to the environment.

When you start to think in population terms, normality and adaptation are assimilated. Isn't it strange then that officially these psychotherapies are the best valued by government systems since they are close to medicine and education due to their corrective and normalizing nature? That's the question I ask the system.

Today, we can also see the continuity of these approaches with mental hygiene, which made its ideal of health the "social efficiency" (Lopera: 2012). It is quite different from what was proposed by the post-war WHO when it clarifies that the impulse to adapt to the environment is not in itself healthy and that, on the contrary, the healthy thing can be to change the environment.

It should be added that, in recent years, the same North American Academic Psychology, with the emergence of Positive Psychology, has shifted the horizon from adaptation to happiness, which otherwise seems to be the new object of public policies and the economy.

A correct life and a healthy mind produces a happy subject. Adaptation and happiness, then, could be the keys to defining mental health in official terms.

We could hardly deny the importance of a healthy organism of the capacity to respond to the environment's challenges in terms of adaptation. And happiness is in the Greco-Roman bases of Western culture, as what the human being can aspire to.

The question that arises, however, is because of the utilitarian connotations of this behavioral science. It evolves from a conception of the human being typical of said philosophy to a concern for the human being's usefulness as an instrument and drifts towards behavioral engineering. In the words of G. Canguilhem, the question that arises is: where do these psychologists want to go by doing what they do, and what role could a definition of mental health play in this?

Going back, it is necessary to recognize the impact of humanist psychology – the so-called 'Third Force' – in the United States itself and the world, which undoubtedly had direct consequences for psychotherapeutic work and the notion of mental health.

Although eclectic and quite vulnerable to fashions, humanistic psychology reintroduced the notion of human nature and trust in it. For this reason, each one is called to search within himself, in the real self or the organismic consciousness, the guidelines for a correct life. Mental health, then, is synonymous with congruence and spontaneity. According to what he is, a healthy person lives to the inner truth of his being, not to social roles or calculations of utility.

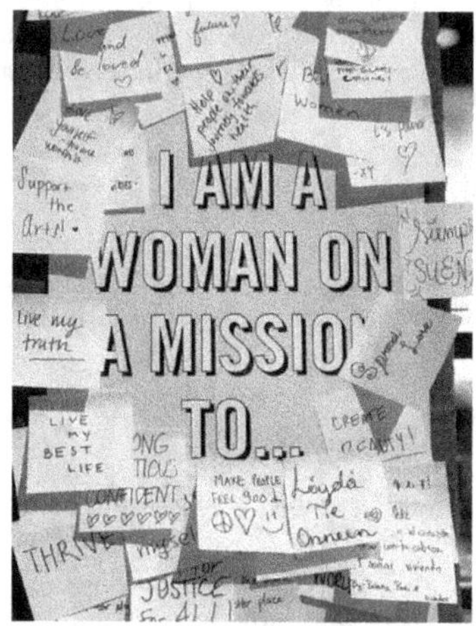

Humanists, in principle, depart from the adaptive and normalizing ideal of the psychotherapies of the 1950s. And rather, they seem to promote a return to classical ethics, to a dimension at least, which is not that of moderation, but rather that of doing what is following the ultimate nature as the way to be happy.

Living in harmony with your nature, that is, health. And with the arrival of transpersonal psychology, it is no longer just living in unity with our nature but living a life in union with the cosmic reality, destiny, or a kind of higher consciousness. The psyche is thus restored to its spiritual condition.

However, a somewhat different nuance arises when adding the notion of self-realization, so dear to humanist psychology, to the definition of mental health. The actualization of each one's potential as a key part of health is in different definitions of it. In contrast, mental health is inevitably impregnated with a developmental paradigm and the modern notion of progress.

Terms such as "grow as a person" or "personal development" are inseparable from the North American humanist current, which is usually interpreted as aspiring to more, having goals, going beyond the satisfaction of needs.

And it is that what we can understand as personal fulfillment is different in a worldview where everything has a place and tends towards something. What terms such as self-regulation, self-development, harmony, happiness, etc. imply. It will vary according to the cultural context in which they are promoted.

By way of synthesis and exaggerating things a bit, we can group psychotherapies, above the theories on which they are inspired, in two types of practices, and that point to two different types of mental health.

On one hand, some are inserted in a tradition that we can call ethical, or "spiritual," in the use that Michel Foucault makes of the expression in the course he dictates between 1981 and 1982 at the *College de France*, whose objective is close to something that we can call "practical wisdom."

On the other, psychotherapies that are better assimilated to medical or psychoeducation routines and whose objective would be to achieve the normalization and adaptation of the subjects to the social environment.

For the former, and continuing with Foucault, what is at stake is the subject's relationship with the truth and its transformation.

For the latter, what is at stake is the functionality of the individual. For the former, someone mentally healthy is someone who knows how to live their life.

For the latter, someone healthy is someone useful.

It is difficult and probably irrelevant for the former to objectify and measure mental health, even more so in a universal way.

For the latter, the concept of mental health can be conceived as a list of properties or characteristics according to a prototype that, if carefully examined, is beneficial for a given social, political, and economic system.

I am sorry if you are confused.

One issue that should cause some surprise within the health field is that many times, mental health is accompanied by expressions such as: "citizenship," "human rights," "democracy," or "social exclusion."

As has already been said, the boom in mental health begins with the post-war period and the need to generate political and social orientations that guarantee social peace. For this reason, it is not surprising that the First World Congress on Mental Health, which was held in London in 1948, had the motto: "Mental Health and Citizenship of the World."

We must not lose sight of the fact that mental health is part of the effort to create a new world order as we know it today. And the slogan of this new order is "biopsychosocial well-being" as a guarantor of peace.

The very concept of mental health has become political rather than technical or scientific. It is something that those critical movements that are born as an alternative to asylum psychiatry, either to disown the notion of mental health or to make use of it. It is about picking up without drama as a pivot to disregard the approach to mental problems and underline its link with social, economic, and cultural conditions.

Antipsychiatry, Social Medicine, and Community and Liberation Psychology in Latin America revitalize the concept of alienation, but no longer as the mental alienation of the 19th century, but as social alienation.

To define mental health, the individual-society relationship is again brought to the front. But the focus is no longer an individual maladaptive to the social environment, but the other way around. For example, a society that creates conditions for an alienated existence.

For this reason, on the horizon of these movements, there is the old idea of freedom. The mental is defined as a consequence of socio-economic structures, the material environment, and cultural life. Mental health is conceived "recursively related to the notion of global capital within a framework of rights and human development, as a problem of political and economic well-being." (Restrepo & Jaramillo: 2012, p. 206).

In the name of mental health, individualism and capitalism are criticized and dictatorships, discrimination, and inequality.

However, what is meant by mental health is rarely said. There is a little theoretical reflection on the concept. In practice, everything fits: interpellation to the State and state plans and programs, work with citizen associations, therapeutic communities, educational workshops, self-help groups, research-action, investigation statistics, etc.

As a theoretical infrastructure, there is considerable flexibility and eclecticism, resort to several concepts, such as self-confidence, self-esteem, empowerment, resilience, social capital, relational capital, psychosocial stress, quality of life, protective and risk factors, etc.

In general, there is more emphasis on action than on theory. Transversal is that it maintains a critical position towards biomedicine and a medical system of the assistance type, approaching public health due to the promotional and preventive emphasis. And due to the community discourse, it is increasingly aligned with official policies and epidemiology.

What is not clear among such an abundant repertoire of actions is what, specifically, it is that it is trying to promote. Perhaps without noticing it, it is implicitly ascribed to a physiological conception of mental health. Simultaneously, the pathogenic consequences of modern life are denounced, elements of the social and economic system that would be harmful to the individual, and general discomfort. Furthermore, it has a direct antecedent in Social Medicine and a long tradition in the social sciences.

There is no health without mental health.

Faced with the risk that mental health is reduced to a field of action of specific specialists who attend to a limited number of problems, the World Health Organization has endorsed the motto: "There is no health without mental health."

Although this can be criticized as a tautology or an unnecessary redundancy, we cannot ignore the impact of mind-body dualism in the health sciences and the divorce between the "bio" and the "psycho" and "social," which is not solved by writing the three terms together as if it were a magic formula.

The WHO, in the well-known 2001 World Health Report, says verbatim that mental health is understood as: subjective well-being, perception of one's efficacy, autonomy, competence, intergenerational dependence, and self-realization of intellectual and emotional capacities.

 In the current Comprehensive Action Plan on Mental Health 2013-2020, the WHO defines mental health as "a state of well-being in which the individual realizes his capacities, overcomes the normal stress of life, works productively and fruitfully, and contributes something to their community."

A set of positively valued attributes are collected in a social environment like ours in both cases. However, it is worth dwelling on one particularity: these are, for the most part, questions that would hardly be required of an animal of another species.

Suppose, then, that mental health is what makes the difference between animal health and human health. It was only pertinent to speak of mental health for the human sphere. It would already be the first decision.

 If so, mental health would be nothing more and nothing less than the human dimension of health. What would make the difference between a veterinarian and a doctor dedicated to the homo sapiens species? It inevitably leads us to philosophical anthropology. Since we would have to discuss what it is, that makes us human.

And it also brings us to psychology, since the historical separation between the field of the natural and the human, the world and the self, which incidentally enables the modern sciences to take off, leave medicine in charge of the bodily machinery.

Now, as there is not one psychology but several, we return to what we pointed out above, there is not only one way to approach mental health from psychology.

If mental health is a *complement* to true health, that of the body, there is a more or less easy way out of dealing with the *true illness* and the state of mind of the person who suffers it. That would be a possible translation for the slogan 'there is no health without mental health' and what is usually done in medical services.

 However, it could go further and make that phrase an attempt to change the dominant conception of health. It would try to stop dissociating disease and sick, and for the same reason, to question an essentialist and reifying conception of diseases. And that no longer looks easy.

Everything that is constructed as 'evidence' today supposes an ontological conception of the disease. And in practice, the subject is no more relevant to the medical act than the setting for a play would be.

Under the heading of mental health, there is a huge amount of research, data, texts, projects, conferences, funds, etc., which is not consistent with the scant reflection on the notion of mental health itself. And it is even legitimate to think that it cannot be otherwise.

Many distrust the concept of mental health, as it always goes hand in hand with promoting a social ideal. And many times, with the attempt to measure and objectify something that is inevitably subjective, which could be inappropriate and even dangerous (Canguilhem: 2004). At the other extreme, there would be those for whom it makes no sense to talk about mental health since it can only make the body sick and heal.

Both positions have arguments in their favor. And yet there are numerous advocates or even activists for mental health. In the name of mental health, most of them seek to improve living conditions and promote democracy, equality, and human rights.

Health is an unquestionable ideal in our society and one of the few foundations that can be used to establish regulations and make changes in the economic, productive, and political fields. In this sense, the concept of mental health would have a strategic value as an argument in the political struggles of the so-called progressive sectors.

It could also have strategic value in attempts to curb biomedical colonization of the healthcare field. However, all this has its reverse. On the one hand, it is very easy to instrumentalize mental health to promote a type of subject with functional characteristics to a given political or economic system.

The great totalitarianism of the first half of the 20th century did. But we can also suspect that capitalist democracies use the concept of mental health to describe, in the end, a good worker and a good consumer. On the other hand, it is easy for daily life to be medicalized in the name of mental health. In other words, as a political instrument, it is a double-edged sword.

Chapter 4: The advent of empathy and emotional intelligence in our lives

Empathy, much more than putting yourself in someone else's shoes. We define empathy and explain why it is an essential quality for your life.

Empathy is one of the most important competencies that are included in emotional intelligence. The word comes from the Greek words that mean "inside him" and "what he feels." However, this psychological phenomenon's real meaning is even more important than the ability to put oneself in someone else's place.

What is empathy?

Empathy is the ability to understand the emotional life of another person, almost in all its complexity. This does not necessarily mean sharing the same opinions and arguments that justify the other person's state or reaction. It does not even mean agreeing with the interlocutor's way of interpreting emotionally charged situations.

Empathy refers, among other things, to active listening, understanding, and emotional support. Also, empathy implies having enough capacity to differentiate between others' affective states and the ability to take perspective, both cognitive and affective, to the person who expresses his emotional state to us.

It's components

Perhaps you have not felt heard on some occasions due to a lack of feedback, support, or understanding. On many other occasions, you may feel that you have not been able to adequately and empathically attend to the emotional state of the other person and ask yourself:

What do I need, or should I do to be more empathetic?

Fundamentally, the components of empathy are the following:

1. Know how to listen

Pay attention to what the other person explains or argues, pay attention to non-verbal manifestations, as it would be in the case of gestures that correspond to the state of mind that is verbalized and do not interrupt the verbal discourse.

Besides, reflect on what the other person is communicating to you and express active follow-up signals as feedback: look at the face, nod your head, or reflect facial expressions congruent with what the other person is explaining to you.

On the other hand, it is necessary to show interest by asking details about the conversation's content.

2. Interpret non-verbal cues

It includes the transmitted messages of a paralinguistic nature, such as intonation, response time, volume.

3. Show understanding

We can show a harmonious understanding of what they explain to us through phrases such as: "I understand that you acted like this. "I understand how you feel." "The truth is that you must have had a great time" ...
The emotions of the person who expresses them should not be invalidated, rejected, or judged, as this is a fundamental premise to show empathic sensitivity.

4. Give emotional help if needed

It is important always to ask our interlocutor if you need any kind of help. However, on many occasions, simply by actively listening to the other, we allow them to "air" and manage their emotional state. In this way, he is relieved to have a reliable listener to whom to convey his emotions.

When the person who listens empathically has lived an emotional situation similar to the one expressed, the communication process is more fluid since there is a greater emotional harmony.

Why practice emotional intelligence?

- As an emotional intelligence ability, empathy is important because it makes it possible to experience various advantages.
- It enables you to appreciate social relationships by interacting more with peers, coworkers, or family groups.
- It makes you feel better.
- Facilitates settlement of disputes.
- It predisposes others to support and share.
- Increases charisma and appeal.
- Let's be politer.

Developing expertise in teamwork, negotiation, and cooperation, as well as becoming better regarded by others.

How can empathy be cultivated?

Empathy practice allows us to widen our viewpoints and enrich our world with new thoughts, points of view, and possibilities.

As we have already shown, it is a vital social ability that helps us listen better, comprehend, and ask better questions, three essential aspects of effective communication. Furthermore, it is one of the pillars of establishing powerful and enriching relationships.

You can incorporate three simple, practical exercises into your routine to improve your empathy.

1. Ask and show interest

Start any meeting or conversation with open and personalized questions: How are you? How about at work? How is the project you started doing? How were your vacations?

Showing closeness and interest in the other person leave room for them to open up and simply receive.

2. Read theater scripts

Read theater scripts and focus on one character. Search the text for what is beyond words; The personal history, previous experiences, the fears it hides, its desires and illusions, the emotions on the surface.

3. Choose a person

Choose a person at random and try to find out what moves them through their non-verbal communication (emotion and thought). A good time to carry out this exercise is in public transport, in a cafeteria. These places are rich in scenes as they can be used to put empathy into practice.

Are you empathetic? Ten typical traits of empathic people

Are you an empathetic person? Know that you also have some difficulties in dealing with it.
The characteristic feature of empathic people is that they know how to put themselves in others' shoes and understand their emotions and physical symptoms. They are extraordinarily sensitive people.

Their vision of the world is very intuitive. They relate to others prioritizing their emotions and sensations over calculation and coldness. They usually find it difficult to describe and put into words everything they feel.

Empathy: a quality to develop

Being an empathetic person is something positive for life. But it also has quite a few less desirable points. People with this trait may also be more vulnerable to the emotional impact of things around them.

For example, they may be more prone to anxiety attacks, depression, chronic fatigue, and other symptoms and disorders related to emotional instability.

However, empathy is a virtue that can help us a lot throughout life, especially if we learn to manage it effectively. The first step is to know if you are an empathic person.

The ten traits of empathy

This section describes the ten characteristic features (habits, attitudes, and behaviors) of people who have highly developed empathy.

1. They are more sensitive than other people

Empathic individuals are detached, open to new experiences, kind, and good "listeners." They are attentive people and know how to transmit these good feelings when communicating with others.
They are always ready to help and offer a shoulder to cry on. But they can also be hurt and offended with amazing ease. They are very sensitive people, to the point of being truly susceptible in some cases.

2. Empaths "absorb" the emotions of others

People with high empathy are influenced by other people's emotions and humor, for better or worse. They can feel what others feel more vividly than ordinary people, which can sometimes be difficult to overcome. If they are around someone anxious or stressed, it is hard for them not to have their minds emulate those attitudes. Luckily, they are also infected with positive emotions.

3. They are usually introverted

We can refer to the difference between introverts and extroverts. In the case of empathic people, it is often the case that they tend to be quite introverted. They don't enjoy large parties too much, preferring small groups or going out for coffee with a single friend.
Even among empathic subjects who are more open to going to parties and places with many people, they tend to be careful and prefer to moderate the amount of time they spend in these types of environments.

4. They are more intuitive than average

Empaths perceive the world through their intuition. They like to develop their intuition and listen to their hunches regularly. This allows them to surround themselves with positive people and get away from those who may upset their emotional balance.

5. They like to spend time alone

They are very sensitive people and tend to be affected if they are listening and helping others for a long time. For this reason, they periodically need to be alone to return to their emotional balance.

6. They can overprotect themselves in romantic relationships

Living with a partner can be complicated for an empathic person, and they can even develop Philophobia or similar manifestations. They avoid falling in love with someone, so they don't have to suffer later if things don't go quite right.
They may be afraid of being emotionally swallowed up by their partner. They need to redefine their concept of love relationship to have positive and happy relationships.

7. They are easy prey for emotional vampires

Have you heard of emotional vampires? They are those people who have a bad habit of unloading all their negativity on other people, from whom they "suck" their energy to continue in their spiral of fatalism, anger, and resentment.

Empathic people can especially suffer the effects of having an emotional vampire around, as they are especially vulnerable to all the bad feelings that these individuals convey.

8. They feel very comfortable in contact with nature

The obligations and stress of daily routines affect us all, but especially empathetic men and women. They tend to disconnect and recharge their batteries when surrounded by nature: climbing mountains, enjoying a sunny beach or simply strolling through a green meadow.

9. They have the sensations on the surface

Empathic people are more sensitive in general. They can feel very bad in noisy surroundings or when they notice that there is a lot of tension in the environment.

10. They are good people, even to the detriment of their well-being

Empathic individuals are good people - they have big hearts and sincerely care about others. They feel bad when they see someone suffering on the street, and they cannot help but attend to them to try to mitigate their pain.

Although it is an undeniable virtue, the truth is that empathic people can go too far and become obsessed with dealing with the problems of others and feel frustrated or confused if they cannot solve their problems.

Manage empathy

As we have seen, empathic people have a series of virtues associated with other problems for their emotional well-being.

Some techniques can help these people to manage their personalities and not be greatly damaged by their sensitivity. Controlling time and schedule, setting boundaries with people who need help, and habits like meditation and mindfulness can restore psychological well-being.

In this busy world we live in, in which we are constantly connected to new technologies, the mind jumps from one place to another continuously, scattering our thoughts and emotions, making us feel stressed, nervous, and even anxious.

The way of life in Western societies puts us on *automatic pilot*, which means that days go by without noticing what is happening inside or around us. We are pulling, walking through life, without stopping for a single moment to observe ourselves internally, without stopping to think about our needs. Always ruminating, clinging to expectations rather than reality.

Living on autopilot, a bad option

Living on autopilot, living by inertia, and being carried away by routine can be very comfortable in the short term. It's easier for the days to go by, and don't face the fear of talking to your partner about how you feel. Or is it less complicated to get carried away from day to day than to admit that you are sad, right? The planets will align to solve your problems.

But living far from the present, that is, with the armor on and without feeling anything, can be negative in the long run, because when something happens, that shakes us (for example, we are fired from work or our partner leaves us), then we have to step on with feet on the ground. Also, living up to expectations can make us wildly unhappy.

Mindfulness: more than techniques, a philosophy of life

More than a set of techniques to be in the present moment, mindfulness practice is a philosophy of life, an attitude that must be adopted to reconnect with oneself. It is a coping style that boosts personal strengths, helps self-regulate behavior, get to know each other better, and creates an environment conducive to well-being.

In other words, mindfulness is a conscious and intentional way of tuning in to what is happening within us and around us and allows us to unmask automatisms and promote integral development.

A few minutes a day is not so much...

For some people, those who live eternally stressed, finding 5 minutes a day to connect with yourself can be difficult. But investing 10, 15, or 20 minutes a day for your well-being is not so much.

As already mentioned, the important thing in this discipline's practice, regardless of the techniques used, is to adopt the Mindfulness attitude, which promotes attention in the present moment, without judging, and with compassion towards oneself and towards oneself and others.

5 Mindfulness exercises for greater well-being

Before going to the list of exercises, it is important to note that practicing mindfulness, being an attitude towards life, is not limited simply to performing these exercises but is a way of dealing with the events that occur in daily life. Still, adopting a healthy habit like this is beneficial for many reasons.
With that said, here is a list of practical Mindfulness exercises:

1. Mindfulness in a single minute

This exercise is ideal if you are starting to practice mindfulness as you progress in learning mindfulness. It is ideal for increasing practice until you reach about 15 or 20 minutes a day. Also, because it only takes one minute, this exercise can be practiced anywhere and at any time in your daily life.

2. Landing breath here and now

This exercise is ideal for turning off the autopilot. By practicing it, your attention is focused on the present moment and stops the constant flow of thoughts, memories, images, or ideas. It is ideal for discharging the accumulated tension in a very simple way.

To do this, you need to focus your attention on your breath. A gentle, deep, and constant inspiration should be taken through the nose. When filling ourselves with air, immediately release the air through the mouth with intensity but without forcing the throat. Noticing a distraction (which is normal), we observe what caught our attention, and we return to the breath.

3. Mindfulness breakfast

It is common to get up in the morning on autopilot. You get out of bed, shower, get dressed, eat breakfast, brush your teeth, and another day at work. Yes, another day!

You can break this negative habit by doing mindfulness in the morning. So you will face the day differently. For this, you must sit in a quiet place and turn off the television so that you are silent. You must also have the mobile away. It's about not having distractions. When you get ready to have breakfast, try to focus your attention on the flavors, smells, the touch of food, or drink... feel them! In this way, you will be with your attention in the present moment, and you will see the difference.

4. Attention to the sounds of the moment

This exercise consists of consciously observing the sounds that occur in our environment. Therefore, it is about staying listening, hearing them as they sound without identifying them, judging them as pleasant or unpleasant, or thinking about them. Without any effort, sounds are observed, and other external perceptions are put aside. When noticing a distraction, we observe what captured our attention, and we return to listening to the sounds, relying exclusively on the breath of that moment.
When listening to sounds that enter our ears, thoughts, and feelings related to what we hear arise. This exercise tries to know silence and sound in a not conceptual way (without thinking) but experientially (feeling them).

5. Body scanner

With this exercise, we try to get in touch with our body's experience as it is, without judging, without rejecting the unpleasant sensations or sticking to the pleasant ones. This exercise is also called a body sweep or body scan.

It is necessary to sit in a comfortable position, with an upright back, although it is also possible to adopt the lying position. Then close your eyes, pay attention to your breathing, and walk through your body. This type of meditation is advisable to be guided.

8 Mindfulness activities to improve emotional health

A selection of practical mindfulness exercises for both children and adults.

Mindfulness, or mindfulness, is one of the most useful tools to achieve emotional balance and improve people's concentration and well-being.

Its effectiveness has been scientifically proven, and there is increasing evidence that its use helps regulate emotions, reduce stress and anxiety, help you sleep better, and promote creativity. Mindfulness is also enriching for those healthy people without psychological imbalances, who simply want to live their life more fully.

This ancient practice allows you to be in the present moment. It is a coping style that fosters personal strengths and helps to be more aware of the immediate experience with a non-judgmental, open, and accepting attitude. Mindfulness helps self-regulate behavior and promotes self-awareness, as well as creating an ideal environment for well-being.

Mindfulness activities for greater emotional balance

But more than a set of techniques to be in the present moment, mindfulness is a philosophy of life. This attitude must be adopted to reconnect with oneself and be more aware of the reality surrounding us. It requires practice and will, so it is necessary to carry out a series of activities to improve the ability to be in the here and now with a non-judgmental and compassionate mindset.

There are many exercises for this purpose. Below you can find a series of mindfulness activities for children and adults.

Children can also get started in mindfulness practice. In this way, they develop this habit that will help them know each other better and relate better to the environment to be happier in the future.

1. Bee breathing

The Bee Breath, or Bhramari Pranayama, is a simple but very effective exercise to focus attention on the breath and to free the mind from agitation, frustration, anxiety, and get rid of anger. Since its practice is not very complex, it can be done anywhere and even at an early age. It consists of covering the ears, closing the eyes, and exhaling the air. It is necessary to pronounce the letter "m" until the breath is finished.

Without a doubt, it is an easy exercise to practice, although it is necessary to learn diaphragmatic breathing to be able to exhale for longer. The exercise can be done as many times as you want, but it is advisable to start with few repetitions and gradually increase them. The sound that results from this action is similar to the buzzing of a bee. That is why this activity is called "Bee Breathing."

2. The art of playing

To perform this exercise, it is necessary to place the children in pairs. One of them is given an object (a pen, a toy, a stone, a ball, etc.) and is asked to close his eyes. The child who has the object describes it to his partner.

After a minute or two, the same process is carried out, but this time, the other partner is in charge of describing the object. Despite this activity's simplicity, it is ideal for teaching the little ones that they can isolate their senses and, if they wish, they can focus their attention to live different experiences.

3. Attention to the hood

This exercise has two parts. The first one consists of ringing a bell and asking the children to listen to the vibration of the sound of it. Little ones should listen carefully and raise their hands when they no longer hear the sound vibration. Afterward, they should be silent for a minute and pay attention to the other sounds heard after the ringing of the bell has stopped.

When the sound ends, the children should be encouraged to share their experiences and say what they heard during this period. This activity works attention and mindfulness and helps to connect with the here and now.

4. Become a frog

Children can learn to practice mindfulness by turning into a frog for a few minutes. Frogs are a clear example of what mindfulness is. Just like when people meditate, frogs remain motionless for a long time. They are rarely agitated but stand still, watching and breathing calmly, and their belly moves sharply with each inhales and exhale. By adopting this amphibian role, children learn to stay still, breathe in a controlled manner, and observe what is happening around them without flinching.

...and for adults

Adults can practice mindfulness in their everyday lives practically anywhere. Any time is a good time to focus on the present moment, adopt a non-judgmental mindset, and treat yourself with compassion.

5. Exercise of the five senses

This exercise is simple and can be applied quickly in almost any situation. All it takes is being aware of our senses and experiencing each of them separately. To perform this activity, you just have to follow this order:

- Look at **five things you can see**. Look around you and pick something you wouldn't normally notice, like a shadow or a small crack in the ground.
- Observe **four things you can feel**. Become aware of four things that you are feeling in the present moment, such as the texture of the pants, the feeling of the breeze on your skin, or the smooth surface of the table where you are resting your hands.
- Look at **three things you can hear** and focus on the sounds around you. For example, a bird, the refrigerator's noise, or the sound of traffic on a nearby highway.
- Notice **two things you can smell**. Pay attention to smells that you are generally unaware of and see if they are pleasant or unpleasant. The smell of nearby pine trees, of the beach if you live on the coast, or of a fast-food restaurant near your house.
- Observe **the taste of your mouth**. Focus on the taste of the present moment. You can sip a drink that you have on hand, chew gum, eat something, and even taste the taste of your mouth without ingesting anything.

This is an easy exercise to practice that can quickly take you to the here and now. How long you spend with each sense is up to you, but each object of attention should last a minute or two. The idea **is not to do meditation but to return to the present with an improved state of consciousness**.

6. Active listening: observe non-verbal language

This activity is ideal for developing active listening skills, a form of communication that requires an effort on the part of our cognitive and empathic capacities. The receiver is not a mere receiver of the words of the sender. Many times, we think we are listening when we are hearing.

Active listening is not listening to the other person but being focused on the message that the other individual is trying to communicate. It is being in the here and now with full awareness. We focus not only on the speaker's words but also on what they are trying to convey through non-verbal language.

To perform this exercise, it is necessary to get in pairs. One member has two minutes to explain a pleasant experience in their life or an opinion on a recent event, while the other actively listens. What do your eyes, your posture, or your gestures say? Do you seem proud when you tell? Does it convey passion? The receiver has two minutes to observe the non-verbal communication of his partner carefully. After finishing the exercise, both share their experience as active listeners.

7. Mindfulness eating

With the rhythm of life, we have today, it is usual that we do not stop for a moment to connect with ourselves, not even when we have a few minutes to eat, because either we turn on the television or we are thinking about what we have to do this afternoon. Well, it is possible to practice mindfulness while we eat or have breakfast. To do the mindful eating exercise, you simply have to pay full attention to what you will eat.

You can start by focusing on what you are holding. Observe the feeling of what you have in your hands (for example, a toast or a fork). Once you know the texture, weight, color, etc., focus your attention on the smell. Finally, put the food in your mouth, but do it slowly and with full awareness. Notice the taste or texture as it melts in your mouth. This activity can help you discover new experiences with foods that you frequently eat.

8. Attention to the center of the image

To carry out this activity, it is necessary to view the audiovisual content shown below:

This exercise's objective is simple: to focus attention on the point that is visualized in the center of the image despite the changing color pattern around it, which can become distracting or provoke unwanted thoughts. It is an ideal exercise to start in the practice of mindfulness and become aware of the thoughts that come to mind and are sometimes not aware.

This exercise aims not to get lost in these thoughts, which can be very pronounced in people prone to anxiety. This experience is similar to the phenomenon of silent fixation that results from staring at a candle flame.

Work and organizational psychology: a profession with a future

Psychologists in companies, their functions, and their importance for the health of corporations.

Many students start their degree in psychology, thinking about dedicating themselves to clinical psychology. Still, as the profession progresses, they find that dedicating themselves to that field of psychology is increasingly difficult. One of the areas with the greatest career prospects is the psychology of work and organization, of which many psychologists become part of a company's human resources department.

However, human resources and organizational psychology are not quite the same, and becoming a specialist in human resources is not a prerequisite for becoming a psychologist. On the other hand, in addition to the human resources department, an organizational psychologist may perform his duties at the management level or in the field of commercial research and marketing and even development.

In today's section, we will review the organizational psychologist functions, and we will delve into the differences between it and the human resources professional.

The work or organization *psychologist*, also known as *an industrial psychologist* or business *psychologist*, is a professional who applies psychology principles in the organizational and works environment.

To do this, he has studied mental processes and human behavior (both individual and group) and puts into practice his training for problem-solving in the workplace. Its general role encompasses the study, diagnosis, coordination, intervention, and human behavior management within organizations.

You can work as part of the company as an employee within its organizational chart (for example, in the selection and training department). However, sometimes, you can work as part of an external company outside the organization. Performing functions of evaluating the performance, work environment, and health of workers or offering coaching services for employees or managers, among other functions. Some organizational psychologists choose to develop their professional careers as scientists or teachers.

On the other hand, this concept is closely related to work psychology, although some nuances differentiate them. As its name suggests, organizational psychology focuses on the interactions between individuals, those who make up a team, a company, a department, etc. On the other hand, work psychology focuses on work dynamics, that is, the application of strategies and behavior patterns to start from a series of available resources to obtain a specific and objectively observable result: a product, a plan, a service, etc.

Functions of the work or organizational psychologist

The organizational or work psychologist has an important role in three main areas:

- **Human Resources** (education, training, etc.)
- **Marketing** and Social and Commercial Research.
- **Occupational Health and Safety** (Occupational Health Psychology)

But what are the functions it performs? Some of the functions of this professional are the following:

- **Plans, organizes or directs various functions within the organization**, such as recruiting, evaluating, compensating, retaining, and developing people.
- **Observe, describe, analyze, diagnose, and resolve conflicts** in human interactions. In this way, it ensures a good work environment and develops the organizational culture.
- **Analyze and modify the physical, social, and psychological elements** that affect job performance and impact employees' efficiency.
- **Apply questionnaires and interviews for the correct diagnosis of the climate**, productivity, and occupational health, and carry out preventive actions to correct possible imbalances.

- **When necessary**, advise the scorecard regarding collective bargaining, possible business strategies, improvement of corporate image, etc.
- **Analyze and put into practice different psychological techniques** to increase productivity, improve the organizational climate, avoid fatigue, and anticipate accidents or occupational health problems, such as **burnout.**
- **He contributes his knowledge as an expert in leadership styles**, interpersonal relationships, emotional control, negotiation techniques, decision-making, or correct planning.
- **It uses tools for talent detection and organizational development improvement** and conducts studies on consumer needs.
- **Recommend and implement actions to incentivize, compensate, and remunerate** staff and ensure their well-being, safety, and occupational health.
- **He is in charge of the training area and designs training programs** for staff development and career and promotion plans.
- **Directs and executes the personnel selection processes**. To do this, you can use different psychological tests and questionnaires to detect the candidates' competencies.
- **Analyze the needs of the staff**, the job, and the organization.

Differences between the occupational psychologist and the human resources professional

It is common to refer to the organizational psychologist as the human resources professional when they are different. The organizational psychologist is a psychologist who has specialized in the field of organizations and work, while the human resources professional may not have training as a psychologist.

The subjects taught in this career include occupational psychology subjects and other subjects, such as labor and trade union law or taxation of individuals.

This occurs because in the human resources department of a company, personnel selection or training functions are carried out, and collective negotiations or tasks such as payroll management can be carried out. The organizational psychologist's profile fits into some areas of this human resources department, but not all.

Organizational psychologist training

Suppose you are a psychologist and want to dedicate yourself to organizational psychology. In that case, you should know that an organizational psychologist, unlike the human resources professional, has completed a Degree in Psychology. Some psychologists finish their degree and then start working as recruiters or recruitment technicians. After learning about the world of human resources, they are trained to cover other HR areas, such as personnel administration or labor law.

Others, on the other hand, after finishing the Degree in Psychology, decide to do a master's degree. If that is your intention, you must choose between taking a master's in human resources management or a Master's in Organizational and Work Psychology.

While the first one trains you on issues such as budget, personnel payments, and expenses, labor legislation, contracts, labor rights, worker safety systems (avoid accidents) selection, and training, the second allows you to study the behavior of the individual within an organization and everything related to motivation, leadership, stress (and other work-related illnesses), work climate and culture or the influence of psychological variables on performance.

The most common psychological problems in top executives

These are the most common psychopathologies among senior executives and managers. People under high pressure are more likely to develop certain psychological disorders. This is the case of senior executives, managers, and other highly responsible positions.

Below we will compile the most common diagnoses that usually occur in this type of person due to their jobs and lifestyle characteristics.

What are the most common psychopathologies among senior executives?

Executives, managers, and other profiles of the highest business level are subjected to daily routines that facilitate the appearance of a series of pathologies. Let's see what the most common psychological problems in senior executives and related positions are.

1. Anxiety

It is not surprising that the first psychological pathology that we encounter when talking about people who live by and their work is anxiety. These individuals will tend to live in a constant state of alert, continually anticipating possible situations related to their work environment and the decisions they have to make to always achieve the best results.

This over-activation, logically, is not something that the body or mind can endure for a sustained time without a series of consequences, some physical and others psychological. The most common psychological symptoms of anxiety are a constant feeling of guilt, worry, and overwhelm. Sometimes you can fear the loss of control and even think that you may die.

Among the most common psychological problems in senior executives, anxiety causes these people to be restless, irritable, have trouble concentrating, and feel like they forget some things. They can also experience blockages at the motor level, which feeds back anxiety, establishing a vicious circle.

2. Depression

Depression is, along with anxiety, one of the most frequent mental disorders. Hence, it is logical to think that it is another of the most common psychological problems in senior executives. It is not uncommon for the two to appear together since the Anxious-depressive symptomatology is one of the pictures that psychologists often find in their consultations.

Depression is characterized by **a mood of general sadness, feelings of guilt, and unhappiness**, sometimes due to a traumatic event and other times without a clear cause, but which can perfectly fit with an exhausting lifestyle that ends up exhausting the mental defenses of the individual. The case of senior managers would be a profile in which this disease could emerge if the necessary precautions are not taken to avoid it.

3. Obsessive-compulsive disorder

Another of the most common psychological problems in senior executives would be OCD or obsessive-compulsive disorder, which would be related to anxiety disorders but with very specific characteristics. Hence the DSM-5 diagnostic manual gives it a category Independent. In this case, **people develop a series of irrational obsessions that they try to appease through compulsive behaviors**.

These obsessions or circular thoughts saturate these individuals' minds, preventing them from focusing on other issues normally, so they develop rituals or compulsions to try to leave those thoughts behind and be able to focus on the issues that concern them. For a person like a manager who needs his mental capacity to the maximum, intrusive thoughts represent a big problem.

OCD is not a disease that affects as much population as anxiety itself. Still, it is common for those people who have a greater propensity to suffer it to see it even more facilitated by a high level of stress maintained over time, which is precisely the lifestyle that a manager usually leads. Hence this is one of the most common psychological problems in senior executives.

4. Narcissistic personality disorder

The fourth psychological alteration that we would find would be a narcissistic personality disorder. In this case, we are talking about a psychological alteration that affects the person's personality that **makes him perceive himself with importance beyond what it corresponds to**. The individual who suffers from this disorder usually believes himself to be the center of the world, with qualities few or no one else possesses.

Not only that, but you need others to make you see how special you are so that compliments will be almost a requirement. This feeling also **causes him to consider that his rights are greater than those of others**, and therefore he will expect better treatment than anyone else, simply because he is who he is.

You will have little or no empathy and expect your subordinates to be 100 percent involved in company tasks, regardless of their personal lives, health, or other issues. Indeed, it is a profile that could fit some senior managers in some companies, so narcissistic personality disorder could not be absent as one of the most common psychological problems in senior executives.

What elements of the professional context generate these alterations?

After addressing the most common psychological problems in senior executives, we must know the bases that make these people have a greater tendency to suffer certain pathologies than the rest of the population. We are talking about **the profile of a person who usually works many more hours a day than would make up a typical workday**, which is generally 8 hours.

On the other hand, these individuals may spend 10, 12, or even 14 hours in the office. It is also common for them to move between different venues, sometimes internationally, which implies traveling by plane, sometimes even changing time zones, with the consequent jet lag. Timing is everything, and they generally rush from one place to another to get to all the meetings on time and have several on the same day.

Besides, **this implies a very poor sleep**, supplemented with large doses of coffee, which only acts as a patch, since nothing works the same as restful sleep. Not only is it the lack of sleep, but it is also that this situation is usually accompanied by fairly improvable nutrition, because sometimes because not a single minute of work is wasted, the intake is done very quickly or sometimes it does not even take place, which is even worse.

As if that were not enough, the issues dealt with at the work level on a day-to-day basis are highly sensitive, involving making decisions of enormous significance, which can mean a rise or fall in the company's stock market, million-dollar profits or losses, and achieve closing deals essential with other companies or even have in their hands the possibility of winning or losing projects that involve many jobs.

Handling all of these issues constantly is something that not all minds are ready to do. Even the strongest can suffer a series of consequences, which are some of the most common psychological problems in top executives and which we have previously seen in detail.

The last factor would be that of free time. **The disconnection from work, so important to clear the mind after a tiring day at work**, many executives do not have. Endless days at the office are followed by moments at home in which this person does not disconnect. You use your phone or computer to answer calls or emails, review documents, or try to move forward on different projects.

The same thing happens during the holidays. These individuals never really disconnect from work because they think that their tasks are essential for the company, and therefore they do not usually take days off. If they do, the same thing happens when they get home: they are watching their laptop or their smartphone, so they simply move their workstation to another location.

This factor also affects their personal and family lives. Sometimes they have problems getting involved as much as they would like and thus enjoy more time and with better quality, for example with their children, their partners, their friends, etc. This could enhance the discomfort that the person already feels with the situation, as it would affect him to involving third parties.

In summary, I am talking about people with responsibilities of the highest level, who travel constantly, sleep little, do not have healthy eating habits, hardly know how to disconnect, with hardly any vacations or free time with their own family. It seems like an extraordinary breeding ground to generate a whole series of pathologies that we have seen, representing the most common psychological problems in top executives.

Chapter 5: Emotional intelligence in design and marketing

Cartesian dualism has marked our way of understanding emotion as an independent aspect of mental processes. The latest studies in the neurological field allow us to understand the fundamental role of emotions in information processing. This section reviews the latest trends in marketing, advertising, and design that reflect this new way of understanding the brain.

The new currents of *marketing* and communication, such as *one-to-one marketing* or relationship *marketing*, have raised trust as a theoretical basis to foster friendly relationships with consumers.

This new way of understanding *marketing* is based on four trends that have been decisive in the genesis and conception of unconventional communication: interactive communication, relationship, loyalty, and permission.

The goal is to achieve customer loyalty always to buy the same brand because they are convinced of their superiority over the competition. This ideal situation is increasingly difficult to achieve since the products are more like each other, and the differences are hardly noticeable:

The fading of the product identity of the product due to the constant technological change intervention that continuously modifies it already the loss of objective differences (in their components, their applications, etc.) between the goods of different manufacturers.

The consumer takes the product's quality for granted and wants to trust a brand that offers guarantees. For this reason, companies consider it more profitable to keep current customers, who already know the product, than to convince potential customers through large advertising budgets.

In this sense, the brand is constituted as a set of intangibles that give meaning to the product's material value.

The brand's main role is to create and spread a universe of significance around a social object (be it a product, good, or service). This brand universe confers personality and character to the product, which allows us to differentiate it.

Thus, decide more in line with our scale of values. Even certain brands have created such a solid universe that they arouse both sympathies and antipathies in society, thus equating themselves with political parties or religious institutions. For this reason, more and more brands are made up of subjective attributes, also called emotional:

Normally these values are defined in opposition to the materials or functional and receive different names according to the authors. We can designate them as "implicit, subjective and immaterial values" or as "sensorial-emotional experience" and simply as "emotion."

From this point of view, emotional values are built independently of the functional value of the product. This responds to a classic conception of the relationship between reason and emotion, as opposing values can never be combined, as autonomous functions of the brain.

However, scientific advances in recent decades, especially in the neurological field, have shown that emotional processes take place in the brain, in the same way as rational processes, interacting with each other,

For this reason, an analysis of emotion is essential as a transversal concept of the brand, from the design of the product to its communication. To do this, we must know the origin of the importance of emotional values in the communicational field and its implication with other disciplines such as neuroscience and industrial engineering.

Humanization of communication

The beginning of applying the so-called emotional values in the advertising campaigns of the big brands is the result of a deeper process of change that has changed the way of conceiving the consumer-company relationship. This treatment tries to imitate certain aspects of personal relationships based on trust and mutual respect. Both concepts are key in new disciplines, such as customer relationship management and permission marketing.

The humanization of communication is a real trend that is present in the main current theoretical currents. This coincides with the explosion of new technologies that offer users the necessary power to exercise their right to reply. Tools such as the Internet and the mobile phone have fostered interpersonal relationships by overcoming distance and space barriers.

The maximum expression of this trend is viral *marketing*. This communication strategy aims to professionalize traditional word of mouth by using interpersonal communication tools, especially email and mobile phones.

The main evidence of this fact is the proliferation of *marketing* campaigns viral and the birth of advertising agencies specialized in communication. However, this professionalization has led to a certain deviation naturally and spontaneously in which messages are spread. In this way, some brands offer material rewards to those who speak well of their products; others go further: they carry out orchestrated campaigns. They hire people who walk around with the product as regular consumers.

This manipulation could affect the confidence of the issuing source to the extent that there is an interest in launching the message.

Although *viral marketing* is not the subject of this section, it serves as an example to show how companies seek new ways to achieve a lasting relationship based on trust. This shows the difficulty that some brands find to connect with their consumers.

One of the traditional mistakes made by companies in their market analysis is the consideration of their target audience simply as a consumer of the brand, forgetting that they are people and customers.

In short, what has marked the beginning of a new stage in current communication is the passage from the importance of the product to the importance of the person, from the rational to the emotional. Although Levitt already stated in the 60s in his famous section "*Marketing* myopia," where he highlighted the error of many companies when defining the objectives of the company, focusing more on the characteristics of products than on the needs they satisfy.

This humanization of communication strategies is a reality that today we can verify simply by contemplating any advertising *spot*, where more and more we find brands that seek identification with a series of global values, such as freedom in the campaigns of the telecommunications company Amena or the emotion in those of Movistar.

The consumer: the brand evangelizer

In contrast to this trend towards the humanization of communication, some authors maintain a new type of customer that is more demanding and concerned about the responsibility of their commercial actions. This would mean thinking that people act rationally and thoughtfully when deciding to buy any product or service, considering its characteristics. At the same time, this contrasts with the lack of time and lack of interest, which forces decisions to be made quickly and without thought.

The excess of information and the lack of time to convert that information into true knowledge provoke in people a state of anxiety called information anxiety.

Is the customer as rational as we think? Do you make decisions after considering all aspects of the products or services you purchase? In general, we can say that the degree of involvement in the purchase decision process will depend on the type of product, its price, the associated risk, the frequency of purchase, and of course, the personality of the buyer.

This perspective on consumer behavior comes from cognitive psychology, which has limited the analysis of emotional implications.

However, studies conducted on *merchandising* show that around 70 percent of decisions are made at the same point of sale, which shows that certain purchases are made in very short periods. This limitation would prevent considering all aspects to make the best decision.

In short, when a person discovers a need and decides to satisfy it, a process of searching for information begins where the opinions of others acquire a certain relevance, especially when there is the necessary degree of trust.

At this point, a new type of consumer appears, which completes an opinion leader's concept. Toffler coined the term in his work *The Third Wave* (1980), where he refers to a new agent of the global village, which is not limited to its role as a consumer but can also provide other goods or services network.

The term's evolution has allowed the integration with other concepts and tendencies until resulting in the conception proposed here.

According to the study carried out by the advertising agency Euro RSCG, *Prosumer Pulse 2005*, "the prosumer is a proactive person, eager for information and opinions, who actively shares his views and experiences with others."

They are people with leadership and persuasiveness who actively live the brand and who want to spread their message because they feel it as their own. This communication ability is what differentiates the consumer as the traditional opinion leader.

Although this new dimension of the concept is somewhat far from the origin of the term, the truth is that the consumer, as described by Toffler, is also a person who anticipates events intending to adapt his offer to the needs of the applicants, seeking mutual benefit.

What differentiates these people from the rest is their ability to adapt to new situations. This flexibility is a characteristic of emotional intelligence.

Emotional intelligence

As we discussed at the beginning of this section, the latest studies on brain activity have discovered the true importance of emotion as a key factor for the human mind's proper functioning. As Damasio points out in his classic work, *The Error of Descartes* (1996), body and mind act as an inseparable set that interacts with the environment.

This allows us to understand that reason may not be as pure as most of us think or wish it was, that emotions and feelings may not be intruders at all in the bastion of reason: they may be entangled in its networks, for the worst and the best.

This accredited Portuguese neurologist demonstrates this fact by studying cases of patients with brain injuries who are unable to lead a normal life despite keeping all their cognitive abilities intact. In short, people have lost certain basic abilities to live in society, including planning time and the future. These skills are not usually measured on intelligence tests.

This very limited view of human intelligence has worried certain psychologists like Goleman, who has proposed a broader approach that includes the study of so-called emotional intelligence. As stated in his work, emotional intelligence is a way of interacting with the world that takes emotions into account and includes impulse control, self-awareness, motivation, enthusiasm, empathy, and mental agility.

Although, as a psychologist, Goleman focuses on knowing how to control human emotions to improve social and personal life, his physiological analysis finds that the functioning of the human brain is not always rational.

This author wonders, "how can we be so rational at one point and so irrational the next." This is explained by his conception of the human mind, made up of two perfectly combined pieces, the rational and the emotional. However, certain events can affect this gear, which could throw the balance to one side.

The emotional mind is characterized by its speed and clairvoyance, which allows us to make decisions at critical moments, a key fact for human evolution. Of course, the emotional brain is influenced by social and cultural contexts. Could this explain impulse buying decisions? Are consumers emotionally intelligent people?

In general, it would be interesting to deepen to what extent the emotional and rational minds work in parallel in the purchase decision process. In other words, Cartesian dualism has had consequences such as a vision of the purchasing decision process focused almost exclusively on the rational mind, an antagonistic approach to advertising strategy, which must choose between rational or emotional axes, when in fact, they are two aspects of the same reality.

The best example of emotional intelligence is the state of flow, which, if we remember as a state that represents the highest degree of control of emotions in the service of performance and learning.

A state in which people are absorbed by complete and undivided attention to what he is doing, and his consciousness merges with his action (Goleman, 2004: 145-146).

In principle, anyone could achieve this maximum degree of emotional control through attention and concentration. The goal is to overcome barriers of attention and focus on work so that we can overcome ourselves.

Saving the distances, the specialists of *one-to-one marketing* try to achieve this maximum attention by personalizing communication and interaction with the user. In short, create a relaxed atmosphere where the brand is founded with leisure and entertainment activities.

Imagine for a moment that someone has entered a website and is so drawn to the site, both for its content and its design, that they forget why they got there. He's fine. He likes what he sees, plays, reads, downloads games… In short, he lives the brand in a relaxed and pleasant environment.

Neuromarketing

Neuroscience is a new discipline that studies the human brain's functioning when it tries to assimilate any stimulus through advanced techniques. Among them, tomography allows us to see how and where the human brain acts in the face of external stimuli.

Therefore, *neuromarketing* supposes the application of the advances of this discipline in the field of *marketing*. According to Braidot, "its purpose is to incorporate knowledge about brain processes to improve the effectiveness of each of the actions that determine the relationship of an organization with its customers."

The latest studies carried out in *neuromarketing* showed that some product preferences, such as the eternal dispute between *Coca-Cola* or *Pepsi,* are more related to the right hemisphere, precisely where the emotion is located.

Scientists at the Baylor School of Medicine in the US have found that the decision between Coca-Cola and Pepsi is not due to their taste but also to the brand's emotional and cultural issues. The experiments' results were surprising since participants who did not know which brand they were drinking activated a different region of the brain than those who did know the brand.

In the first case, the participants opted for Pepsi, and the region activated as the ventromedial prefrontal cortex related to the basic desires in the reward processes. This refers to taste.

On the contrary, when they knew the brand they were drinking, the volunteers leaned for Coca-Cola.

Other parts of the brain related to changes in behavior moved by emotion and affect were activated (hippocampus, midbrain, and dorsolateral prefrontal cortex).

Although it should be noted that the tests were conducted with non-carbonated soft drinks because the scanners do not recognize carbonated drinks.

Although most of the sections consulted on this concept, generally of an informative nature, do not make special mention of the methodological issue, there is an excessive triumphalism in this regard. When they refer to the methodological question, it is superficial or too optimistic.

When a new technique comes to verify what scientists have been trying to decipher for several decades, you must be cautious. Not in vain, advertisers, especially creatives, have been trying for a long time to connect with the most emotional part of human beings. It seems that with the scientific rigor that surrounds this type of discipline, advertisers and designers will have an "infallible" tool to know the effect of your creations.

But they are still experimenting that need a calm reflection on their methodology and their results. Meanwhile, specialized consultancies and advertisers with enough financial capacity to assume the risks have already emerged.
As José Luis León affirms, the function of advertising is to create a climate of trust and closeness with the target audience, leaving aside the more technical and rational aspects, more typical of the business world.

However, advertising, in its search for the prediction of human behavior, has joined forces with research, a field dominated by systematization and rationality: advertising is an excellent territory in which, like no other, they live in conflict with art and science that has always enjoyed their territories, usually mutually exclusive, have been forced to coexist in the advertising universe strangely.

For this reason, *marketing* professionals, closer to research and results from measurement, are very attentive to advances in neuroscience. However, ad creatives have not been surprised by these discoveries, as they test the human brain's complex workings with the results of their campaigns.

However, despite their search for emotional truth, their creative possibilities will be diminished. All this, if finally, the experiments in *neuromarketing* give good results to predict human preferences.

Emotional usability: Kansei engineering

The design has also suffered from this dualism between reason and emotion. Proof of this is the conflict between art and functionality that certain projects of little professionalism generate. From our perspective, both functional and aesthetic values are configurative elements of any design application, from graphic to interactive.

In this sense, we must remember that design, beyond its application to any discipline, tries to communicate messages to a set of people (target audience) with a series of specific characteristics. In this way, Wong refers to the designer's task: A good design is the best visual expression of the essence of something, be it a message or a product. To do it faithfully and effectively, the designer must seek not only for that something to be confirmed.

This can also be applied to website design, which in its obsession with applying usability principles, has neglected other aspects, such as the creativity or personality of some brands in their virtual presence.

Traditionally, the Internet has been considered a cognitive medium, and from this perspective, the accessible and functional website has been created, considering the Internet user as a rational user.

However, sometimes some websites are successful despite not complying with the principles of usability. For this reason, design professionals are reviving an old imported concept of industrial design: *Kansei* engineering.

This discipline, developed in Japan by Mitsuo Nagamachi in the 70s, focuses on studying the quality of an object to produce pleasure when it is used. Design also seeks to apply emotional values to products' production: Can a product express an emotion? Can a car connect emotionally with its audience? To this type of answer, the emotional design or *Kansei* tries to respond.

This Japanese word refers to sensitivity applied to product design.
Eastern culture has traditionally been concerned with the balance between mind and body. And it seems that their products reflect that philosophy that pampers the aesthetics of the product without forgetting its ultimate goal.

Kansei engineering is a method of incorporating emotional variables into product design. A way of systematizing what until now has been considered uncontrollable: emotions. Can the appearance of a product provoke emotions?

Although the use of this term was limited to experts in industrial design, its application to web design has generalized its principles, until it has become a discipline with its characteristics that have even led to usability experts, such as Norman (2005), revised his treatises to incorporate emotional values. This supposes creating a discipline with its entity that receives different names: emotional design, emotional usability, among others.

In summary, we could say that the products with the highest aesthetic value seem easier to use than less attractive ones. Indeed, it is a question of perception because "the emotional system is capable of changing the operational modality of the cognitive system" (Norman, 2005: 34).

Norman explains brain entanglement through three interacting levels of processing: the visceral level, before thought, the behavioral level, which refers to the experience of use. And the reflective level, where understanding, thinking and concentration function mediated by cultural, social, and personal preferences. Each one requires a different design, but they must be considered together if they are satisfied at all levels.

Quick and stereotyped judgments characterize the visceral level. In this sense, the visceral design aims to highlight those attractive physical characteristics at first glance before thought acts. The result could be very basic but eye-catching products with "very intense and bright primary colors."

Regarding the behavioral level, we are especially interested in the physical sensation of the products, the noise of an engine, or the sensation of robustness when closing the door of a Volkswagen brand car.

A study by Millward Brown demonstrated the importance of sensory experiences in branding, which can lead to higher sales. The study's objective was to create an inventory of sensory impressions for a selected set of brands to detect how users experience these sensations and how they can affect their relationship with the brand.

Finally, the reflective design is the most complex as it refers to the meaning we bring to objects, situations, and people around us based on our educational and cultural level. At this level, the brand's image and its positioning in the mind of the consumer works. It is a personal matter that comes from individual experience with the product, so an enriching contact with the brand is essential. At this level, are the brand communities and? Prosumers? Skillful to communicate that experience and recommend the product or service to other people.

Although, as we have pointed out before, the object of desire may not be the product itself, what we imagine ourselves doing with the product, which ultimately inspires us.

Desmet distinguishes between *A-emotions*, that is, those emotions caused by the characteristics of the product (colors, aesthetics, materials) that correspond to the visceral and behavioral levels proposed by Norman; and *R-emotions*, that is, those emotions motivated by what the product represents and inspires (reflective level) that are based on the representation of the product, on what we imagine we will do with it.

Although, from our perspective, we consider that it is a combination, normally, we tend to like a product for its color, texture, and aesthetics, in short for its design, but also because we imagine what we will feel when using it. All this is because the cognitive and emotional levels work in a network, interacting with each other, and modifying our perception. The first, being tangible, has interested the experts in *Kansei more to* find some valid method to incorporate these variables from the beginning of the product design. In this sense, some brands have already incorporated some of these concepts into their design processes, especially the automotive sector, where the differences between benefits hardly exist, making it necessary to distinguish the car by its design, by its brand. Mazda is one of the brands that has put these concepts into practice and has proven its results with the MX5 model, a convertible that has become one of the world's best sellers.

Scientific advances on the human brain's functioning have shown the high involvement of emotions in mental processes. The relationships between the left and right hemispheres explain the complex web of attribution of meanings to what we do, think, or buy. For this reason, brands would have to incorporate all these concepts from product design to *marketing* and communication strategy to manage the entire consumer experience.

Emotional intelligence and the awkward side of web design

Emotional intelligence is described as the ability to generate empathy with others, putting ourselves in their place. Day by day, technology becomes much more humanized. And platforms offer an increasingly personalized user experience.

In this sense, the programming and web design of the different digital products must strive to find a way to have "emotional intelligence" and connect with users.

Twitter celebrated its 10th birthday in March 2016. It was a day of pride for the organization and all of its supporters. It launched a fun heart button/animation to make the day amazing for its users.

It was amazing, but the animation went way too far as soon as the day ended. Some people didn't care, and others didn't even notice, but there was a hole left behind for those who did. This is not an exaggeration; with confetti, the heart bursts bounce and is cheerful and vibrant. Overall, the boring activities of liking or preferring a tweet made it much more interesting and enjoyable.

Let's talk about the look of hearts vs. stars as well - if you remember, Twitter changed its user interface from stars to hearts in late 2015. "The heart is a universal symbol, a symbol that is far more inclusive,"

Casey Newton said. Take a look at what the new Heart UI is all about in Twitter's gif. (No, it has not been the same as the confetti explosion since his birthday.)

Since Twitter was involved in increasing interaction for progress, the decision was business-oriented. But how does the heart react adequately to a negative comment? It's not; it's pointless and insensitive. Often a star is worthless, which is exactly why it matters.

Not only is it a Twitter problem, it doesn't have anything to do specifically with Twitter, but it's a perfect example. What if there was a horrible news accident?

By generating more forms of answers, Facebook manages this dilemma. Providing emotionally intelligent responses is still very difficult for a social network, but the acceptance of multiple responses by Facebook is a step forward.

Siri doesn't know how to deal with this either, because we're in it. In critical cases, there are several posts on Siri that do not provide practical support. However, Apple offered useful responses and actions for rape victims and concerns about suicide via a software update in April 2016.

The intelligence of emotions and architecture

Beth Dean wrote an excellent Medium post about traumatic encounters that technology unwittingly brought up. The blog post was inspired by a website that asked her if she knew her deceased mother while trying to verify her identity (it's absolutely nothing compared to making a simple animation). Beth talks about designing from her viewpoint. Emotional intelligence, with. With five traits: self-awareness, self-regulation motivation, empathy, and human ability, she described emotional intelligence.
Knowledge of oneself and self-regulation
Facebook offers a perfect example of self-awareness, asking a user to see advertising based on their conduct. It provides not just a great user experience. It is more important to the user.

As a smart strategy for numbers, Dean explains self-regulation. Just because the numbers are going up doesn't mean that it's all right. A website that spammed the contacts of a user to improve their interaction was the example you used. Of course, interaction improved, but as soon as the customer realized that they approached their contacts reluctantly, trust in the business decreased. That is why you see the message, "we will not publish on your behalf" when you visit a site via a social network such as Facebook, Google, or Twitter.

Motivation, empathy, and talents of humans

It is a little difficult to understand motivation, but it comes down to the users' perspective and their particular context. It's about trying to make the target audience understand and not disrespect others who are not. You don't want your app to feel rejected by anyone. A little modesty can go a long way when it comes to empathy.

That leaves us with the abilities of humans. When it comes to tech, what a fascinating concept to speak about, don't you think? Human abilities apply to the general tone used by the product and the external environment it projects. It is about useful, but also a suitable material.

We need to be mindful of these aspects to develop and program systems and goods for a more human experience.

It is possible to see empathy and emotional intelligence as software seeks to be inclusive. In her post, Dean states that she is now very used to "tech personalities" and recognizes that software is designed for the majority. To include all possible scenarios, the most impressive software can, therefore, be developed.

Chapter 6: The Black Dog

Sir Winston Churchill, the former Prime Minister of the United Kingdom who steered the country towards Second World War victory, struggled from depression. He metaphorically called his depressive state, "a black dog."

Such a metaphor is widely discussed over the internet. In the context of this chapter, we are going to shed light on psychological techniques and proposals on "leashing the blackdog." In other words, controlling and minuting symptoms of depression.

We start by exploring different theories that explain depression.

The theory of response styles: this is how it explains depression

This theory, proposed by Susan Nolen-Hoeksema, talks about the nexus between depression and rumination.

In Psychology, many theories have been proposed to explain the origin and maintenance of depression: learning, cognitive, social theories.

Today **we will** learn **about Susan Nolen-Hoeksema's theory of response styles**, a cognitive-social model that alludes to the subject's reflective style to explain the emergence of depressive disorder.

Some people turn things around a lot, even going into a loop and doing absolutely nothing to remedy their problems. We are talking about a ruminative thinking style. But how is this style of thinking related to depression? We will see it next.

Theory of response styles

The theory of response styles is a theory encompassed within cognitive-social models **proposed by Susan Nolen-Hoeksema (1991, 2000), an American psychologist** and professor at Yale University. When Nolen-Hoeksema began the studies on ruminative style, she found that **ruminative thinking and depression** did not show significant differences between girls and boys during childhood.

However, from adolescence, both elements' presence was double in the case of women, remaining constant during the rest of their life cycle (Nolen-Hoeksema, 1991).

The author alluded to the factors that determine the course of depression. According to the theory of response styles, **how the subject responds to the first symptoms of depression** influences its duration and severity.

The theory does not explain the origin of depression, if not its maintenance and exacerbation.

The ruminative style in depression

Ruminative style or rumination are repetitive ideas about sadness itself, its causes, and possible consequences. It is a predictor of some psychopathologies and is linked to depression, as Nolen-Hoeksema suggests.

Also, it can be considered a type of coping strategy in situations of stress and discomfort. However, it is considered dysfunctional and maladaptive, **reaching consequences as serious as suicide, in extreme cases**.

According to the theory of response styles, once you have depression, focusing attention on the symptoms and their implications without doing anything to alleviate them (exhibiting a ruminative response style) will maintain or exacerbate depressive symptoms.

This style is the opposite of an active style based on distraction or problem solving, which would be functional and adaptive.

Numerous experimental and field studies support the theory of S. Nolen-Hoeksema and affirm that a ruminant response style in a subject **increases the probability that a depressed mood will intensify,** even becoming a depressive disorder.

Ruminant style mechanisms

The theory of response styles raises a series of **mechanisms that explain the negative effects of the ruminant style**, which are the following:

1. Vicious circles

Vicious cycles occur between depressed mood and the **negative cognitions** associated with depression. These two elements influence each other and feedback, causing depression to become chronic and accentuate.

2. Decrease in the generation of effective solutions

The generation of solutions aimed at solving basic problems is practically nil.
Thus, **the subject does nothing or practically nothing to solve his situation**. He simply "turns around"
what is happening to him, without reaching any conclusion or putting any solution into practice.

3. Interference with instrumental behaviors

The ruminative style negatively interferes with instrumental behaviors that would provide reinforcement
and a sense of control to the subject.

In other words, rumination will hinder the generation and implementation of such behaviors; in this way,
the subject **will enter a state of helplessness and hopelessness** that will lead him to "do nothing."

4. Weakening of social support

Social support is reduced or disappears due to the patient's behavior, which **provokes criticism and
rejection among his family and friends**.

Origin of the ruminant style

The ruminative style that the theory of response styles raises is originated by learning in
childhood, **through modeling and certain socialization practices** that do not provide a more adaptive
repertoire of behaviors.

Results in experimental studies

Ruminative responses have been investigated in experimental studies, and the following effects of having
a ruminative thinking style have been observed:

- Increase in negative and global attributions.
- Increased accessibility of negative memories.
- **Pessimism and biased negative interpretations**.
- Generation of poorer interpersonal solutions.

On the other hand, it has also been seen how rumination can be a predictor of anxiety symptoms, in
addition to depressive symptoms, in individuals with or without pre-existing depression.

The link between depression and perfectionism

How is the tendency to be perfectionism and the probability of having depression associated with each other?

Depression is a very common alteration of mental health, and this is, among other things, because this emotional state is not reached by a single route but by several.

Depression is sometimes discussed with the assumption that it is simply an illness and that, as such, it is caused solely by biological complications in the person's body. Still, the truth is that personality traits and lifestyle habits can explain a good part of our propensity to develop this disorder.

This section will focus on **the relationship between depression and perfectionism**, two highly studied psychological phenomena in which points of interconnection have been seen. And it is that many times we tend to associate perfectionism with a positive and useful aspect of the personality (and to a certain extent). In excess, it can compromise our mental health in different ways.

What do these concepts mean in psychology?

First, let's clarify the concepts that we are going to talk about. Depression is **a mood disorder characterized by a lack of energy and motivation, low expectations, and a state of sadness or anguish** that makes it very difficult to enjoy life's pleasant experiences (a vacation, dinner at a good restaurant, etc.). As a psychological disorder, its presence not only implies discomfort but also negatively affects the quality of life of those who suffer it and increases the risk of suicide.

On the other hand, **perfectionism is scrupulous when evaluating the product of our actions**. This means that we pay attention to the need to do things right and that the idea of creating something with one or more imperfections causes us discomfort.

The relationship between depression and degree of perfectionism

Different ways are tending to a high degree of perfectionism are associated with the probability of having depression. Here we will see several of them, although one thing must be borne in mind: being a perfectionist does not mean that this trait will generate a depressive disorder. Sometimes what happens is that what leads us to develop perfectionism also leads us to develop depression.

Differences between types of perfectionism

First, a distinction must be made between two types of perfectionism: **perfectionist aspirations and perfectionist concerns**. The second of these forms of perfectionism consists of the propensity to worry about the possibility of doing things wrong, the anticipation of failure if we do not pay much attention to what we are doing, and the obsession with avoiding a bad result. However, the first has to do with wanting to be the best version of ourselves and giving importance to doing things in the best possible way.

In this way, perfectionist aspirations are linked to a higher risk of manifesting stress and anxiety problems. In contrast, perfectionist concerns are associated with the risk of suffering from depression.

Those who adopt this type of perfectionism focus their attention on the negative aspect of their skills and abilities and spend a lot of time anticipating and imagining poor results in what they do. The latter fosters emotional fatigue and the inability to enjoy.

Of course, we must not forget that those who follow the path of perfectionist aspirations are not exempt from presenting a greater risk of having depression because **anxiety overlaps a lot with mood disorders**.

Eating disorders

It has been seen that the risk of developing eating disorders, such as anorexia nervosa or bulimia, is associated with a tendency to high or very high perfectionism, which makes sense considering that the discomfort comes from thinking in imperfections in behavior and physical condition.

This is relevant because, **as is often the case with treatable psychological disorders in therapy, having developed one makes it more likely that we will develop another**, and depression is at the top of the list of possible risks.

Work addiction

The tendency to work too much, closely linked to perfectionism, is related to the risk of developing depression in the medium and long term.

There are different explanations for why this happens. One of them is that, as "workaholics" transform their work environment into the main focus of interest in their lives, **little by little, they are cutting off their links with other sources of satisfaction and social life.**

When they find that they cannot keep up with that rhythm of concentration and effort, they find themselves alone and socially isolated, with no stimulating hobbies and, in general, no reason to stop directing 100% of their attention to their work performance. This is the point where depression lands.

On the other hand, the extreme concern to produce and do everything well that causes addiction to work is also linked to lack of sleep, which is most linked to depression if the nervous system does not have time to recover. In contrast, we sleep—the chances of developing mood disorders skyrocket.

How to get out of depression? Tips and effective treatments

What to do when we are going through a time of depression? Going to psychotherapy requires a commitment and effort to change the part of the patient with his reality.

Healthy changes in behavior cannot be made without willpower, effort, and motivation. But ... **How is it possible to be motivated when I feel depressed?** Next, I will indicate some concepts that will help you identify depressive symptoms and tools to combat them.

What to do about depressive symptoms

First of all, it is important to know that to the extent that we are focused on the negative aspects of any aspect of our life. **As we focus on the bad things that happen to us, we take our attention away from the good and positive things**. This ends up becoming a habit for your mind. When depression has been in you for a long time, this connection is so important that you practically cancel out everything positive.

It is sabotage of everything that can be good since your brain automatically looks for something negative to replace it since you have somehow programmed it for that.

One thing I warn you about is that **it is not possible to change the connection and the focus of attention from one day to the next**. But you can start by identifying the things you used to like to do and now don't. As you identify the "negative programming" that you have built with **constant negative thoughts** and behaviors that reinforce it, you will plan new programming with a more positive approach. **Attention** is the ability to concentrate on a particular stimulus that we have selected from among others.

To attend to a stimulus, it is necessary to neglect others. For example, when watching an interesting movie, we turn our attention away from our mobile phone or other things around us. Depression is a disease that collapses people's attention span, and thought processes respond to an involuntary demand for attention.

Therefore, it is important to take stock of the things that are given importance. With therapeutic help, you will be able to change the focus of attention characteristic of depression to recover motivation, illusion, and moments of well-being gradually.

Depressive behaviors take time to settle in your body and mind. It is very likely that this disease's trigger comes from unpleasant experiences or that you do not know exactly its origin. The important thing is to analyze to what extent you have come to program your mind so that the moment of sadness remains established in you.

Why do you get depressed?

Depression is a way to connect with the world and face life. It allows us to constantly remember what could not be done, our defects, what we lack, etc. The difference with a positive connection is looking at all these aspects and, in turn, looking for a solution. Therefore, we would be connecting with things that can be changed. We would begin to change the focus of attention with a balance of thoughts that are not negative.

It is normal, natural, and healthy for you to feel sad at different times in your life.
But when that sadness changes the environment and stops doing the things you like, abandon projects, and despair grows in you, sadness becomes a pathology, so self-evaluation is important to avoid that pathological sadness. Depression continues to take away your moments of enjoyment and well-being.

Get out of depression

It is not easy, but it is possible. If you gradually build a stimulating environment around you, focusing your attention on the positive that you have, and planning activities that allow you to connect with the things you like, things will fall into place.

The depression will fade over time. You must know that, just as depression takes time to set in, you have to be constant in the implementation of positive behaviors to change your perception of the environment. If you don't, depression will take more and more space in your mind and body, going through different degrees of mild, moderate, and severe.

Even in chronic cases, other mental disorders may be associated with depression due to the magnitude of the lack of control of your habits and thoughts. Therefore, it is important to make changes in thought and behavior processes that can influence the creation of an environment that promotes greater well-being and growth.

Depression is a disease that all people can suffer from. Unlike sadness, it is a lifestyle that is adopted with negative habits that are repeated daily, added to the thoughts that allow depression to persist.

You must go to a mental health professional since the techniques described above are only useful strategies that, by themselves, do not replace what a psychotherapy process is. The psychologist will intervene individually in your case to have the necessary tools to deal with your depression effectively.

Behavioral Activation as a therapy against depression

Jacobson (1996) called Behavioral Activation (AC) to the programming of activities, applied together with cognitive intervention techniques, which improve any behavioral deficit or excess in the person. It is **a therapy aimed at treating depression** and understands the behaviors of the person who suffers from it as a symptom and as part of the essence and maintenance of the disorder.

What is Behavioral Activation?

Among the symptoms of depression, one of the most characteristic is inaction, which is part of a vicious circle in which the person suffering from it is immersed: the lack of activity affects the mood. In the same way, a depressed mood produces a lack of activity. This relationship is the epicenter of the Behavioral Activation proposal, which considers some types of depression as elaborate forms of avoidance.

This therapy's objective, framed within the third generation therapies of the cognitive-behavioral current, and which is itself a therapy itself, is that depressed patients can organize their lives and change their environment to **reestablish their relationship with sources of stimulus that provide positive reinforcement for them**.

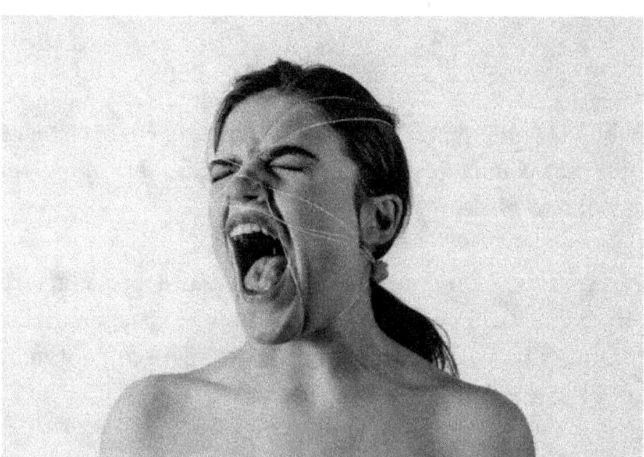

Some of the interventions with behavioral activation methods aimed at reducing depressive symptoms are the prioritization of tasks, the programming of vital objectives, the reinforcement of social contact behaviors, and the performance of rewarding activities.

How does it work?

The therapy is mainly based on **prescribing activities to break the dynamics of inactivity**. To be effective, especially at the beginning, it is necessary that the programming includes easy, rewarding activities (not only pleasant, since we look for activities that are satisfactory and require effort) gradual and that are very well planned, then, especially at the beginning of the program, but it is also easy that difficulties arise for its realization.

Current meta-analytic reviews (Cuijpers, van Straten & Warmer-dam, 2007) and experimental studies in which different therapeutic approaches have been compared - antidepressant medication, cognitive therapy, and behavioral activation therapy— (Dimidjian et al., 2006) have revealed that **purely behavioral interventions are sufficient** for an efficient and effective approach to depressive conditions.

Its advantages

Some of the advantages of Behavioral Activation programs are as follows.

Has shown extensive scientific evidence: Compared with pharmacological therapy, it has obtained comparable results and **a higher percentage of remission in the subjects and adherence to treatment**.

It is a simple treatment to apply: Compared to other proposals, it does not require so many steps.

Does not require modification of thoughts, whose procedure is more complex: The data suggest that the application of the behavioral components by themselves **achieves the same result as full cognitive therapy**.

In short, Behavioral Activation is therapy with strong empirical support, which offers a new treatment opportunity for people suffering from depression.

The four coping strategies for depression

Various initiatives to combat the damaging effects of depression and improve quality of life. Depression is characterized by **maintaining a state of deep sadness** for **more than two weeks, often without knowing why.** Unlike sadness as an emotion, which is transitory and generally caused by something perceived as negative for the person.

To this is added **an absence of pleasure and lack of motivation for any activity**. An alteration in appetite and weight is experienced, since sometimes there is a loss of them, while in some cases the person shows an excessive appetite.

In the same way, **sleep is also affected** by insomnia or excess non-restorative sleep. The person presents fatigue or loss of energy, showing dejection in his face and lack of care in his person, in addition to walking, moving, and speaking slowly.

However, the characteristics of depression are not limited to physical alterations such as those just shown, since the person also experiences feelings of worthlessness and guilt for unimportant things, as if it were a nuisance for the people around him. Inevitably, limitations in mental capacity appear. That is, thinking slows down, and attention and concentration decrease.

Finally, **thoughts of hopelessness appear**, showing apathy towards life, so the person thinks of death as a remedy. According to the WHO, each year, about 800,000 people commit suicide, which represents the second cause of death among young people between 15 and 29 years old.

Coping strategies for depression

What to do when a friend or family member suffers from depression? Let's see.

1. Acknowledge your suffering

First, you need to listen to and acknowledge their suffering. Suddenly, you usually try to encourage the person using phrases such as: "Courage! Don't be sad", "Don't cry anymore," causing guilt and frustration, since it is not something that depends on the person how to feel.

Instead, **when their feelings are validated, and empathy is shown, we become companions**.

2. Don't feed your sadness

It is not about reinforcing their condition by fostering self-compassion or incapacitating the person but treating them as someone going through a difficult time. Likewise, it helps the family member keep busy **with walks, entertainment, small jobs, etc.**

3. Taking any suggestion or threat of suicide seriously

A serious mistake is made when signals of this type are ignored, as the person may be giving a warning. **The best thing to do is to keep an eye on the person with depression**, not leaving them alone for a long time.

4. Seek professional help

At this point, it is very common to only resort to medication. However, despite being useful, it only reduces the symptoms but does not solve depression. So, it is common to find people under drug treatment dealing with depression for a long time: months or more than a year.

Also, the person on antidepressant medication does not begin to notice the medication's effects until two to three weeks after starting treatment. So, **the most advisable thing is to start a psychotherapeutic process to work in the required areas**.

Tips to prevent this mental disorder

These are some recommendations to apply on a day-to-day basis.

1. Do aerobic physical exercise

The chemical and hormonal balance produced by drugs can also be achieved or supplemented with sports and physical activity.

Fatigue is a source of health and good humor since **this kind of exercise produces serotonin**, which is a neurotransmitter related to feelings of pleasure and well-being. It also promotes a state of mental peace, reduces levels of daily stress, and improves self-esteem.

These benefits are better than the most effective antidepressant, and sadly, they are least followed.

2. Avoid isolation

A study (Nolen-Hoaksema and Morrow, 1991) carried out in San Francisco (USA) showed that **isolation favors depressive emotions and thoughts**. It is advisable to have a support network, such as friends or family.

3. Stay busy or busy

Whether outdoors or at home, look for an occupation; that way, the activities will help keep your mind off the thoughts that accentuate depression.

4. Seek professional help

If these tips are not enough, **the psychologist's help will always be the best option to get out of depression**. Proper psychotherapy can achieve the desired results.

Depression is a complex problem, so the recovery process is often slow, so that patience is required from both the affected person and those around him. Although depression often requires psychological intervention, self-help strategies are beneficial for psychological treatment and even prevention.

The benefits of having psychotherapeutic and psychiatric care

What are the aspects of the psychiatric intervention that reinforce psychotherapeutic support?
It is often assumed that psychotherapy and psychiatric treatments are two opposing ways of working, competing with each other to improve people's well-being, and ensure their mental health.

However, the truth is that the idea that these two forms of intervention in patients are mutually exclusive does not make sense. Nowadays, it is known that combining both things helps a lot when treating certain disorders.

In this section, we will see how **having both psychotherapy and psychiatric support** benefits patients and why, in some cases, it is the most recommended option.

Differences between the work of the psychologist and the psychiatrist

First of all, let's see what the aspects in which psychiatric intervention and psychotherapy differ are. Psychotherapy is a concept applied to the need to solve a wide variety of **problems related to behavior, thinking, and emotions.**

This implies that it is not limited to offering services to people who have developed a psychological disorder; for example, some people go to psychological therapy to stop having low self-esteem, improve their communication or social skills, or even better manage couple arguments.

Furthermore, psychotherapy is fundamentally a learning process: patients learn both theoretical aspects of what is happening to them and how they can solve it and practical ones, about how to overcome this problem by adopting new habits and styles of thinking.

On the other hand, **psychiatry proposes resources from the world of medicine** since, after all, psychiatrists are doctors specialized in mental health. For this reason, they work in cases in which there is (or may exist) a disorder, so they care for people whose quality of life is being significantly affected regularly.

It is very common for the use of psychotropic drugs to be proposed, although always strictly following their instructions, since these products may have side effects to be taken into account.

The benefits of having psychiatric and psychotherapeutic support

These are the main advantages of having help in both ways combined, psychotherapeutic, and psychiatric.

1. Psychiatric support helps meet the goals of psychotherapy

Sometimes the symptoms of the disorder that affect the patient are so intense that it makes it difficult for them to reach the goals set in psychotherapy or even prevent them from concentrating and understanding what to do.

In these cases, the use of drugs or other psychiatric tools can allow **you to reach a point where the discomfort is reduced enough to get involved with the tasks associated with psychological therapy**, and from there, continue to improve.

2. Psychiatric intervention helps a lot in crisis

In acute discomfort cases, in which it is a priority to make the discomfort go down as soon as possible, psychiatric intervention may offer somewhat faster ways of action than psychotherapy. And once that phase has passed, **having a psychiatric professional allows you to detect in time the signs that another crisis of this type could arise**.

3. The combined use of both interventions intensifies their effects

On many occasions in which there are severe psychiatric or psychological disorders, the effects of psychotherapy and psychiatric intervention **are mutually reinforcing in terms of patient improvement consistency**. They feel better and more consistently.

4. Psychological support helps to commit to both therapies

Finally, psychotherapy predisposes patients to commit more to their process of improvement and recovery of well-being. Its **effects extend beyond the motivation to continue going to the psychologist** (as long as it is necessary) and include the psychiatric route's commitment.

You are loved. You are needed. You are important. And you matter. That is all this time around from me and Oscar. We hope to catch you soon with another entry. Wear a mask.

"If you have enjoyed reading this book, I would be very grateful if you could post an honest review on Amazon. All that you need to do is to click the blue link next to the yellow stars. On the left, You'll see a gray button that says "Write a customer review"—click that and you're good to go, thank you."

Carl